ENGLISH WITHIN THE ARTS

ENGLISH WITHIN THE ARTS

A RADICAL ALTERNATIVE FOR ENGLISH AND THE ARTS IN THE CURRICULUM

PETER ABBS

HODDER AND STOUGHTON

LONDON SYDNEY AUCKLAND TORONTO

British Library Cataloguing in Publication Data

Abbs, Peter
  English within the arts.
  1. English literature—Study and teaching—
  Great Britain
  I. Title
  820'.7'10941   PR51.G7

ISBN 0 340 28377 7

First published 1982
Copyright © 1982 Peter Abbs

Typeset by Macmillan India Ltd, Bangalore.
Printed in Great Britain for Hodder and Stoughton Educational, a division of Hodder
and Stoughton Ltd, Mill Road, Dunton Green, Sevenoaks, Kent by
Richard Clay (The Chaucer Press) Ltd, Bungay, Suffolk

For my mother and father
in loving appreciation

The province (of the imagination) is to give consciousness to the subject by presenting to it its conceptions objectively.

S. T. Coleridge

I am doing a novel which I have never grasped. Damn its eyes, there I am at page 145, and I've no notion what it's about. I hate it. F. says it is good. But it is like a novel in a foreign language I don't know very well—I can only just make out what it is about.

D. H. Lawrence on 'The Rainbow'

The artist, at the risk of their displeasure, tells the audience the secrets of their own hearts.

R. G. Collingwood

Because a work does not aim at reproducing natural appearances, it is not, therefore, an escape from life—but may be a penetration into reality, not a sedative or drug, not just the exercise of good taste, the provision of pleasant shapes and colours in a pleasing combination, not a decoration of life, but an expression of the significance of life, a stimulation to a greater effort in living.

Henry Moore

Contents

Introduction

Economic recession tends to spell educational regression. It will be extremely difficult in the coming decade to establish any true sense of education as a primary process of the psyche in its quest for meaning and it will be even more exacting to establish a proper understanding of the unique contribution of the arts to education. It is all the more vital, then, that teachers work to clarify the essential meaning of their disciplines. In this book I seek to discover a new definition of English teaching within the arts and of the arts within a comprehensive curriculum. Nothing would satisfy me more than if as a result of its argument English teachers formed strong practical alliances with the neglected disciplines of art, drama, dance, music and film and in so doing developed through creative activity the emotional and imaginative energies of our children and adolescents.

I will argue that the intrinsic concerns of English as a discipline are literary, expressive and aesthetic and that for the best part of a century these concerns have been obscured or, at best, only partially recognized and their full implications invariably missed. This was partly due to the fact that English emerged from classics and unconsciously absorbed many of the habits that characterised the teaching of that subject. It was partly due to English being linked to literary criticism and the historical study of texts with the result that it became allied with the humanities and was seen, therefore, as being more akin to history or social studies than, say, dance or art. It was partly due to the demands of other disciplines which insisted that it was the task of English teachers simply to impart prescriptive grammar, spelling, comprehension, the general skills of language narrowly conceived. From the very beginning English entered the curriculum in surrogate clothing. In the first chapter I will analyse some of these enduring misconceptions. I will also inspect, with more sympathy, the three great traditions which struggled to provide a more comprehensive and demanding understanding of English: the Progressive School, the Cambridge School and the prevailing Socio-Linguistic School. I will claim that while none of these traditions was entirely adequate, each of them formulated certain elements of good practice, and that it is these elements which we must now take into a new synthesis, the radical reconstitution of English as art.

Yet to draw English into the arts is no simple matter. It is, at once, to confront a range of broad generative questions. How is English like art? What is the nature of art? Why is art of educational value? How can art be taught? What is an aesthetic education? It is pertinent to my theme that these questions have not

1

been asked by those forging the dominant theories of English during the last fifteen years. And yet, as I will try to demonstrate, these questions rise naturally out of the teaching of English and would seem central to our discipline. The intention of my second chapter is to raise within English the very questions which it has suppressed. Even to formulate the questions is to gesture to the new ground.

The argument in chapter 2 is deliberately broad because, perhaps over-ambitiously, it seeks to find a common language for art-teaching, a language which is not only fitting for the teaching of English but also for the teaching of dance, art, drama, music and film. Following in the wake of the writings of Robert Witkin and Malcolm Ross, it proposes the need for a common language which has its roots in the dynamics of art-making, in the various phases of the creative act. In my account I am particularly anxious to avoid what might be called the progressive fallacy and struggle to elucidate both the personal and the communal nature of art-making, stressing the reciprocal needs of self and society as they meet in the expressive symbol. In this chapter I also stress the cognitive grasp of the arts. I argue that art is committed to the elaboration of meaning. Just as the sciences and humanities are symbolic forms for the comprehension of experience, so, I maintain, it is with the arts. They are the most sensitive instruments we have for the realization of that perennial decree 'Know thyself and be thyself'. Such an unashamedly epistemological view of the expressive disciplines enables one to perceive their great educational value. If as R. G. Collingwood asserted in *The Principles of Art* it is the power of art to keep consciousness authentic, then it can be seen that art-making and art-responding creates the necessary foundation on which all the other intellectual pursuits can subsequently build. Such an insight is central to the argument of this book.

Having offered a possible language and a broad framework for the arts in education, I consider in chapter 3 the various practical and theoretical implications for English teaching. Here I relate English to the phases of the art-making process defined in chapter 2. The practice I outline depends upon a distinction between English as a medium and English as a discipline. All teachers, simply because they teach through language, are concerned with English as a medium. However, English teachers, as teachers of a specific discipline, are pre-eminently committed to a particular kind of language, the language of literature and myth, the language of feeling and imagination, the potent language of expressive utterance, what D. H. Lawrence named 'art-speech'. In English teaching, by provoking and releasing feeling we engender metaphor and by developing the metaphor, we extend and refine the original feeling. Our concern is with the development of consciousness through expressive symbol-making in the broad context of a collaborative community and an inherited culture. To formulate the aims of English teaching at such a general level is to reveal, again, the underlying arts paradigm. For such a definition can be seen to apply not only to English but to all the other expressive disciplines. However, it is also my intention in chapter 3 to provide immediate and quite practical classroom approaches to English, to present ways of, for example, developing writing and the appreciation of literature.

Chapter 4 concerns the preparation of English teachers. At the moment with English classified as linguistics or social studies (the discussion of 'relevant' extracts culled from literature in the social realist vein), as basic skills or as traditional literature, there are very few courses which cultivate the qualities necessary to teach English as an expressive discipline. Furthermore, students who have studied literature at university for three years are not usually thereby equipped to work creatively in the classroom or, even, in their own discipline. Often an ability to classify and dissect has grown at the expense of the ability to respond intuitively and personally. The student's mind buzzes with critical terminology but the shaping imagination has been paralysed. The abstract response to literature begins with 'O' level preparation, continues into 'A' level and reaches its summation at Degree level. Of course, in some cases, the approach is not uncreative; an engaged conversation between the student and the text does take place. But, invariably, it is deadening and seals off the hidden springs of preconceptual creativity. This means, as I explain in the first open letter in chapter 4, that one has to dramatically initiate English students into the art-making process as soon as they begin their education course. I do not know of many institutions where the emphases are all essentially creative and existential. I have therefore been driven back to offer a personal and dramatic account of the PGCE English course at the University of Sussex. I make no particular claims for this experimental course other than that it is fully committed to the concept of English developed in this book.

Herbert Read in one of his last books *The Forms of Things Unknown* subtitled *Essays towards an aesthetic philosophy* claimed:

> I believe that the kind of illumination that comes to the consciousness of the poet, and is expressed in words, is not essentially different from the kind of illumination that comes to the painter or sculptor and is expressed in visual images; nor is it essentially different from the kind of illumination that comes to the musician and is expressed in tonal images.[1]

It is such a view of the arts, as belonging to a single epistemic community and as being directly concerned with illumination, that lies at the centre of my argument. In the closing chapter I present again the broad argument developed in chapter 2 and consider its educational implications.

Before I conclude this introduction with an acknowledgement of my many and various debts I must finally make a plea for the place of concepts in Education. Part of my argument is broadly philosophical in nature. I hope that my reader will not therefore consider it as being in some way superfluous or as irrelevant to what happens in the daily practice of good teaching. Ideas are, quite simply, indispensable. They are vital because they have the power to engender a play of mind over the actual. They cast a focussed light on settled habits. In the context of teaching, they urge us to see more clearly the nature of our practice. Whether, for example, the way we are teaching is fundamentally sound or whether it is more the product of inertia, of habitual and largely unexamined response. With concepts we can rise above the instant and consider it. The concept is thus a liberating force, freeing us from the mechanical, the inanely repetitive, the fixed routine. But even more than this, concepts can open up new ground – they can suggest the outlines, often hazy, of new territory, territory in which many of the elements are already known to us but in which *the relationship between the elements*, as it emerges through the haze, *is different*, and distinctly so. Concepts not only serve a critical purpose they also have a constructive force. They urge us to criticism. They invite us to imagine. With the use of such concepts as: *psyche, expressive discipline, epistemic community, phases of the art-making process, impulse, representative form, creative mimesis, collaborative community,* I intend to offer my reader a map of the new English as it emerges out of established practices and inherited traditions. I know my reader will not want me to define all these terms in advance. Their meanings will grow from their contexts. However I feel obliged to reflect further on three of the above concepts: psyche, creative mimesis and epistemic community. For these may not be familiar or, even worse, may offend or confound.

Psyche: I use this word as it is employed by analytical psychologists to refer to the four following functions:

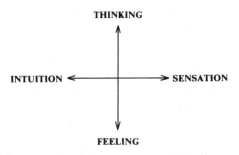

The concept has, I believe, a resonance, deriving from its Greek source, and a complexity, deriving from the above use, which is largely absent from the word 'mind'. Psyche implies that we comprehend our experience not only through the linear, abstract path of thinking but also through our feeling, through our intuition and through our various sensations. To educate psyche is a very different business from educating the mind; it calls for a more profound understanding of knowledge and being. The word psyche, as used by analytical psychology, also compels a recognition of conscious and unconscious modes of expression and behaviour. The expressive symbols of art-making may well have both a conscious and an unconscious purpose and may do their healing work at a depth not open to personal or public inspection. Anyway, I contend that English as an expressive discipline largely exists for the well-being and the continuous development of psyche.

By *creative mimesis* I denote the conscious or unconscious imitation of symbols in the culture in order to express one's personal meaning. The concept embodies a recognition of the reciprocal nature of self and culture, of innovative impulse and informing tradition. The great defect of the Progressive School was that it undervalued the symbolic nature of human existence. It conceived of the individual as though he was a law unto himself, living outside cultural forms, spontaneously creative and self-sufficient. It paved the way to a spurious notion of creativity, a notion which lacked reference to any cultural context, any evolving mastery of form, any adult guidance and criticism. As we shall argue more fully in the following chapters, the Progressive's notion of creativity was spurious because the fact remains that we are born into a community and into culture and that it is only through these agencies that the individual stands any chance of becoming who, potentially, he is. Human life is thus dependent on the gradual mastery of communal symbolism which, if it is healthy, progressively allows for the development of individual experience. Paradoxically, it is partly through the active recreation of symbolic forms that the individual comes to find his own voice. As I will argue in chapters 2 and 3 the concept of creative mimesis has enormous implications for the teaching of the expressive disciplines.

If my reader regards *epistemic community* with some suspicion I sympathise and yet it is a necessary concept, not another piece of educational jargon. It condenses with great economy a complex recognition of the nature of knowledge. Epistemic refers to knowledge and community, in this context, to a common kind of knowledge. In stating that the Arts form an epistemic community I am committed to the notion described earlier by Herbert Read that *the arts are preoccupied with the making of meaning and that the kind of meaning they are concerned with is essentially similar.* The sciences form another epistemic community concerned with a different kind of meaning; the humanities another. Each epistemic community can only be properly understood from within, by reference to its own inherent and unfolding principles. Yet seen together the different symbolic communities reveal man's general quest for meaning through conceptual and expressive formulation. We bring to the world our own symbol-making energies and so recreate it as a distinctly human universe. It is one of the grave imbalances of our civilization that the different symbolic forms have not all been given their proper recognition. For while no symbolic form can possibly possess a monopoly in explanation, the marked tendency has been not only to make science the dominant form, but, furthermore, to judge the humanities and the arts in terms of its prevailing categories and procedures. This has lead, inexorably, to an appalling constriction of the psyche, to the suppression of inwardness, to the neglect of metaphor and the denial of personal meaning. It has lead to the arts being pushed to the very edges of the formal curriculum, consigned, for example in *The Framework for the Curriculum* (Department of Education and Science, 1980) to a vague hotch-potch of ill-fitting bits and pieces (from careers education to technology) yoked crudely together under the title 'Preparation for Adult and Working Life'. To define English as a discipline within the arts and to define the arts as an epistemic community on a par with science, mathematics, and the humanities is to challenge the positivist presuppositions about knowledge and to present fresh conceptual terms for a truly comprehensive curriculum. Epistemic community is, therefore, a necessary concept. With it we can establish the arts as one of the permanent centres of educational activity and show that English teachers, by the very nature of their discipline, must become (with other arts teachers) responsible for such a momentous shift in curriculum matters.

As concepts are rarely invented but more often borrowed and adapted to one's own purposes in an act of creative mimesis so I am indebted to numerous writers and colleagues. In fact, I am indebted to more people than I could possibly name. My intellectual debts are listed in the various bibliographies but I would like to formally thank here those associated with its actual writing. First of all I would like to thank two friends who have been particularly supportive: Judith Keystone (whose valuable criticisms helped me to sharpen the arguments) and Catherine Steward (who tested some of the approaches in her own classroom). As always I must thank my industrious secretary Betty Beytagh for her infinite patience in deciphering and transforming an indescribably messy manuscript. Finally, I must warmly acknowledge the support of the English teacher-tutors working on the University of Sussex Postgraduate Certificate in Education English course and all the English students who have attended the course. The equation is simple: without them there would be no book. I am deeply grateful for their enthusiasm and their criticism, their scepticism and their hope.

1

The Reconstitution of English as Art

I

It is a difficult business cutting through and going beyond what is safely established. Merely to locate what has been excluded in current thinking is taxing, but to take what has been excluded and to bring it into controversial relationship with what is current in order to find a synthesis greater than both, that seems all but impossible to achieve. And yet with regards to English teaching that is now the task confronting us.

In this book my main intention will be to argue for a concept of English as a literary expressive discipline, a discipline whose deepest affinities lie not with the humanities (as has been commonly conceived) but with the arts or what I prefer to call, at least in the context of the curriculum, the expressive disciplines. One of the most important claims I will make is that English should now form strong philosophical, practical and political alliances with the undervalued disciplines of art, dance, drama, music and film. More specifically, I would like to see English teachers turn in a new manner (though, as we shall see, not uninformed by the best in the rich, uneven heritage of English teaching) to the expressive dimension in order to sustain and develop the neglected emotional and imaginative energies of their pupils; and to do this, not in superior isolation (as was often the habit of the Cambridge School of English) but in vivid, open and generous collaboration with those other departments in the school, college or university likewise committed to the expressive and inner life of the student.

For reasons that will become clearer as we proceed, sustained collaborative work and sustained collaborative exchange between the expressive disciplines seldom takes place at the secondary level of education with the result that the arts in our schools have lacked philosophical coherence, organisational unity and practical bite. I think it is not a matter of contention but of simple description to say that no child by design (or, perhaps, even by chance) receives in the state system anything resembling a true aesthetic education. Although one could document many fine exceptions, the expressive disciplines in our schools are in a state of confusion, neglect, poverty, demoralization and absurd fragmentation. The expressive disciplines lie on the very periphery of the curriculum; in most schools they are not even regarded with the traditional suspicion, they are not even noticed. According to formal Department of Education and Science figures, about ten per cent of the total curriculum at secondary level is given to the arts, but, given the way in which many of the arts are actually taught, it would be reasonable to assume that only half of this time is devoted to genuinely expressive tasks, i.e. about five per cent of the total time given to the curriculum is directly engaged with aesthetic experience. Furthermore, in many secondary schools, where an optional system operates after the third year, the arts can and frequently do disappear completely from the education of the adolescent.

I believe that such a dramatic restriction of the aesthetic-expressive dimension calls for a reappraisal of the meaning of English.

At memorable points in the past, as I shall attempt to show, the nature of English has been seen as literary and expressive. From almost the beginning of the century Caldwell Cook linked English with drama and, more generally, with enactment, embodiment and expressive presentation. Under the impetus of what I will name the Progressive Movement in English teaching, innumerable teachers have intuitively felt (rather than conceptually realized) that English belongs most naturally with the epistemic community of the arts. In primary schools, particularly, the connections between literature, song, imagery, painting, sculpture, drama, mime, were spontaneously forged in the practice of good teaching. In this chapter I will critically and sympathetically analyse earlier traditions in the teaching of English in order to salvage some of the elements necessary for its reconstitution. But this will not be sufficient. In order to make our case convincing it will be necessary to examine the dominant theories of the last two decades. This will be contentious, yet it is not, I think, a caricature to suggest that frequently in the last twenty years English has been envisaged either as linguistics or social studies. In the first case, it has suffered from an intolerable narrowing; in the second, from an intolerable diffusion and a dangerous distortion. In both versions English has severed its potentially rich connection with the arts. It is symptomatic of the present state that although English may have reached across the curriculum, it never entered, as an energizing force, the teaching of the expressive disciplines, nor has it given any serious attention to the nature of the aesthetic. Even in the study of literature, there has been a tendency, among leading theorists, to reduce imaginative art to the level of mere sociological manifestation and social class phenomena. These strictures are severe. And are intended to be. Yet it would be grossly wrong-headed not to recognize in the current orthodoxies some major compelling insights into educational practice, into that elusive process we call 'learning'. But this is to anticipate my argument . . .

I am, then, concerned with a revaluation and a reformulation of English. Only by an examination of previous formulations, only by a relentless thinking down to informing principles, can we secure the conditions necessary for the growth of educational disciplines. The practical possibilities not only unfold in the classroom (although what happens there is crucial) they also unfold out of deep insight into living principle, into the intrinsic nature of what it is we seek to do. Paradoxically, if we are to take the chains off the present state of English, we must go back and down, back to half-forgotten formulations, down to underlying principle. This must be the first exercise in any reconstruction.

II

Although, as D. H. Lawrence claimed, logic is far too coarse to make the subtle distinctions life demands, yet in an area as contentious and problematic as English teaching, a few opening definitions are called for. Often the uncertainty of aims which attends English teaching derives from little more than the ambiguity of its own title. For the word English has a number of possible references. Even in its educational context it can possess at least three distinct meanings:

(1) English as a second language
(2) English as the mother-tongue and medium of nearly all teaching and learning
(3) English as a discipline in its own right, as a distinct symbolic form, e.g. English as studied at a University.

In this book I will not be concerned with *English as a foreign language*. I will consider the notion as *English as a medium* and, in particular, the current demand for 'Language across the curriculum' which I will fully endorse. But, essentially, I am preoccupied with *English as a discipline*. Current theories about English tend not to differentiate between discipline and medium, or rather, they tend to dissolve the discipline into the medium. Thus the English teacher becomes responsible for all kinds of language and all kinds of learning. He becomes a general adviser rather than an initiator into a specific kind of knowing through a specific kind of procedure and through a specific kind of language. The English teacher thus becomes like a man carrying a bag of tools but with only other people's jobs to do. Such a view I will argue, while having questionable strengths, is totally inadequate. It leaves out the meaning of the discipline; it discards or demotes the unique contribution English has to make as a symbolic form.

The important distinction I want to establish is that between *discipline* (or symbolic form) and *medium* (the language necessary for nearly all kinds of learning). With this at the back of our minds, we can now turn to examine the three main traditions in English teaching: the Progressive Movement, the Cambridge School of English and the current Socio-Linguistic School. I am going to argue that while no one movement offers a comprehensive account of English, each has offered certain principles, which brought together provide us with most of the elements necessary for a radical yet inwardly consistent transformation of the subject. I will work historically, taking each movement in its chronological order, but, as I have explained, my interests are heuristic and not documentary. I am not concerned with the actual description of the whole rock only the valuable mineral which can be extracted and used in a new context. After all, in education our main concern is the transformation of inherited culture according to our deep existential needs. So, first, we take the Progressives . . .

III

The Progressive Movement in English teaching goes back almost to the beginning of this century. In its early stages (1910–1925) some of its key exponents were: Percy Nunn, Greening Lamborn, Edmund Holmes, W. S. Tomkinson and Caldwell Cook. As early as 1911 Edmund Holmes had written in *What is and what might be*:

> For a third of a century, from 1862–95, self-expression on the part of the child may be said to have been formally prohibited by all who were responsible for the elementary education of the children of England, and also to have been prohibited *de facto* by all the unformulated conditions under which the elementary school was conducted.[2]

Self-expression prohibited. That was the cry and challenge of the Progressive Movement in English. Against the mechanical forms of teaching, the Progressives asserted the need for a freer and more spontaneous approach allowing the child to generate much of the curriculum according to his creative needs. Characteristically, in his book Holmes condemns without qualification the external examination system, complaining 'of its tendency to arrest growth, to deaden life, to paralyse the higher faculties, to externalize what is inward, to materialize what is spiritual' and 'to involve education in an atmosphere of unreality and self-deception'. The critique bears within it its own positive conception of education: as the unfolding and elaboration of self through activity, intellectual enquiry and creative play.

The movement largely derived its thinking from Montessori, Froebel, Herbart, Pestalozzi and, ultimately, from Rousseau. Caldwell Cook's 'Begin with the Child' powerfully echoes *Emile*, Rousseau's influential charter for children. The concepts 'growth', 'self-expression', 'individuality', 'play', litter the works of these early pioneers. As the movement developed so it absorbed into itself ideas from psycho-analysis, particularly from Freud and Jung. It culminated in two highly influential works, Herbert Read's *Education through Art* (1943) and Marjorie Hourd's *Education of the Poetic Spirit* (1949).

The strength of the Progressive Movement was to emphasise the power of creativity in education, to recognize the place of feeling and of imagination, to perceive the value of psychic wholeness. In 1921 W.S. Tomkinson in *Teaching of English: a new approach* referred to reading as 'a creative art' and to the child as a maker who 'strives after the expression of himself and does it in the same way as the poet – by creative work'. Both of these claims remain quite central. It is important to notice also that in this first major move to give English a creative shape, there is an implicit recognition that English belongs with the arts. For Caldwell Cook writing plays, acting, modelling, drawing, painting are part of the same inextricable pattern or paradigm. In *The Education of the poetic spirit* the teaching of drama and the teaching of English are both explored and are seen to be part of the same quest for the symbolic ordering of elusive experience (and thus the refining of that experience). Although there is little conceptual understanding of the nature of the relationship between the arts, there is an intuitive recognition of their common identity so that the teaching of English, drama and even art not only run often side by side but interpenetrate, becoming different facets of the same motion. Fom this practice we have a great deal to relearn. We have allowed specialization and the consequent fragmentation of the curriculum into a thousand jostling bits to destroy the collaborative spirit which should characterise the teaching of similar forms of symbolic activity. Thirty minutes of drama here; one hour of art there; some music somewhere else; lessons of eclectic English scattered throughout the week; we have ended up not with a coherent curriculum but a liquorice allsort confusion. The Progressives were on the right track in emphasising unity and organic form and in intuitively grouping the arts as members of the same epistemic community.

At the same time, it is impossible not to be aware of the crippling weaknesses of the Progressive English teachers. I think it is just to say that they possessed an effusive concept of the child, at once intolerably vague and hugely indulgent. In their minds the poet and the child become synonymous; yet the poet both expresses and extends his own culture in a way no child can possibly do. And, as we shall see in the next chapter, the concept of art as 'self-expression' is severely inadequate. Furthermore there was no critical theory of culture and, while there was a great appreciation of spontaneity, there was no correcting appreciation of critical methods, of ordered and sustained analysis.

There was an inflated view of human nature which gave birth to an almost unhealthy idealism. 'In Utopia', wrote Edmund Holmes, 'the training which the child receives may be said to be based on the doctrine of original goodness'. He saw an 'infinite capacity for good' but failed to detect the shadow which all light inevitably casts. He failed to grasp the perplexities, the irrationalities, the deep ambivalences of the human psyche. This is not the place to explore, in responsible detail, the defects of the Progressive ideology – many of them deriving from that philistine of genius, Rousseau – but those defects weakened considerably the movement I have been describing. At worst, it culminated in a sentimental indulgence of the child's every whim, a building of the curriculum on the sands of chance impulse and immediate gratification. Often it served best as therapy rather than education. And yet in courageously insisting on the primacy of feeling, the Progressives defended the deep springs from which authentic art, whether in English or music, drama or art, derives. The life of impulse was central to the Progressives and it is the key to the expressive disciplines. Without some impulse desiring expression in order to know itself, there can be no authentic art-making. The movement of art-making runs from emotion to expressive medium to symbolic form to the integration of the original emotion and its contemplation. In celebrating feeling, and in placing feeling at the heart of education, the Progressives were responsible for restoring human energies which had been long suppressed and maligned, particularly by educational theorists. In beginning to integrate the formidable and unsettling insights of Freud and Jung into the theory and practice of teaching (as in the case of Marjorie Hourd, Marion Milner, Seonaid Robertson, Herbert Read) they also helped to institute a new kind of understanding about knowing and relating which we have still to develop and make clear. As Marjorie Hourd was the first to recognize, the insights coming from psycho-analysis had a major bearing on the way in which English could be reconstructed, the way in which children's writing could be interpreted, the way in which drama and literature worked, the way in which the English teacher could relate to the injerent ambivalences in adolescent emotion in order to make possible the education of the poetic spirit. Perhaps the great sanity of the Progressive Movement is concentrated in Herbert Read's conviction:

> The secrets of our collective ills is to be traced in the suppression of spontaneous creative ability in the individual.[3]

And yet . . . And yet spontaneity also requires, paradoxically, discipline and a bed of culture. Without form, without tradition, without a fund of exemplary symbols, the creative impulse becomes lean, autistic, exiled. To understand the nature of these complementary qualities we must turn to the next major reconstruction of English, made within a different tradition and in the context of the study of English at University, the Cambridge School.

IV

If the Progressive Movement had its line of descent running backwards from Montessori to Froebel to Herbart to Pestalozzi to Rousseau, that is, into one European philosophical and pedagogic tradition, the Cambridge School, centred on the work of F. R. Leavis, remained stolidly English, running back into the work of George Sampson, Matthew Arnold, and, to a lesser extent, Coleridge. The greatness of the Cambridge School was to keep alive and make muscular the nineteenth century Arnoldian literary-critical tradition. Out of the practice of I. A. Richards, the Cambridge critics developed a critical method, a procedure for reading with sensitive accuracy, feeling and due discrimination, works of literature. They provided, along with T. S. Eliot and Ezra Pound, a more coherent sense of the continuous organic tradition of English literature. In new and worsening cultural circumstances, the Cambridge School gave powerful currency to the notion that the teacher, critic and artist had no choice but to oppose the destructive and seemingly inexorable drift of industrial civilization. As George Sampson had trenchantly written in *English for the English*:

> I am prepared to maintain, and indeed, do maintain without reservation or perhapses, that it is the purpose of education, not to prepare children for their occupations, but to prepare children against their occupations.[4]

This defiant antagonism to the dehumanising effects of the Industrial Revolution permeates the Cambridge School. It issued in an insistence on the need to generate in the young the habit of cultural discrimination and an awareness of the English literary tradition which, in its profound engagement with fundamental human dilemmas and possibilities, embodied authentic alternatives to the crass hedonism and sharp technicism of our own times.

As the Cambridge School owes much of its inspiration and many of its characteristic concerns to F.R. Leavis, it is necessary to attempt here a brief evaluation of Leavis' contribution to English. I will consider, first, what I regard to be the positive aspects of his work, then move to some of the more negative features. I will argue that while the Cambridge School does not provide us with a sufficiently comprehensive concept of English, it does provide us with those elements of criticism and cultural heritage which the Progressives had either ignored or rejected, elements quite crucial to any reconstitution of the subject.

There can, I think, be little doubt that F.R. Leavis was a great English critic, one of the few and one of the best in our century. His greatness, though, rests not so much on the versatility and fertility of his mind, as on its passionate stubborness over a few principles. Here is a critic who knew a few things, we might say, but knew them with the whole energy of his being. This insistence on certain premises, sustained throughout a life-time, confered a narrowness to his writing but within that narrowness there developed a fierce consistency, challenging, disturbing, uncompromising.

Leavis, in the first place and most obviously, believed in significant literature as a formative pressure on existence. Because of this he argued that there could be no division between aesthetics and life, between beauty and meaning. Art comes out of life and returns us (often at a heightened level) to it. The critic holding such a position is often dubbed a 'moralist' or called 'puritanical'. Surely, such a response is evasive, indicating an unwillingness to face the demanding nature of literature, which inevitably intends meaning. For if we consider the nature of language itself, we discover two interdependent aspects, a power to denote and a power to connote, that is, a power both *to refer* and *to express* a feeling about that which is referred to. The writer using language, in a personal and charged manner, will, by the very nature of his medium, fuse both aspects. In insisting on the moral nature of literature, Leavis reminded an age, sinking into the desolate marsh of materialism, of the power of the creative word to promote consciousness and conscience. He had also carried the tradition of moral criticism, which runs from Johnson to Arnold, into our own confused century. This in itself was an achievement difficult to overestimate.

In fact, tradition is a vital concern in Leavis' writing. His criticism points us not to a number of isolated geniuses, but to an organic English tradition out of which humus the great literary works have grown. Leavis constantly reminds us that a writer labours within a context and that there is a crucial interplay between the two. On the one side, the writer keeps the language alert and sensitive, on the other side, the state of the language, which the writer inherits, opens or restricts his range and his impact. Commenting on D. H. Lawrence, Leavis writes:

> Without the English language waiting quick and ready for him, Lawrence couldn't have communicated his thought: that is obvious enough. But it is also the case that he couldn't have thought it. English as he found it was a product of an immemorial 'sui generis' collaboration on the part of its speakers and writers. It is alive with promptings and potentialities, and the great creative writer shows his genius in the way he responds. Any writer of the language must depend on what his readers know already (though they may not know that they know) must evoke it with the required degree of sharpness or latency[5].

The extent to which the writer can advance consciousness, the sensitive, articulate life of the whole man and woman, depends, to a large extent, on the general state of the culture which surrounds him. A sensitivity to the state of the language – to its possible resonances, its underflow of meaning, its implications —are not only the hallmark of the good writer, but also of the good reader, critic and teacher, all of whom work the language in the name of vision, insight, individual depth and adequacy of understanding.

For Leavis there is another important and related condition necessary for the development of the writer. If his work is to develop he requires an audience, a dedicated minority, quick to appreciate his intentions and ready to evaluate them as they are embodied in his actual works. If the writer had such an audience he has, again, secured one of the critical conditions necessary for the evolution of his own talent. Without it, he is liable to disintegrate, to become paranoid, to undervalue the need to communicate, to waste energy in attacking those who will not listen, or even more dramatically, to commit suicide. All of these negative responses have, indeed, tended to mark the arts and to disfigure them since the Industrial Revolution. But in our own century the conditions for symbolic creation have become all but traumatic. According to Leavis, the critical, sympathetic and educated community disappeared in England during D. H. Lawrence's life time. There is not the space – nor is this the context – in which to weigh Leavis' specific judgement. Here it is important to note the intertwined notions of cultural continuity and of critical audience. These I would contend are both central concepts charting an indispensible area neglected or negated by the Progressives in English. The life of impulse – and the life of impulse reflected back to us through art – requires for its development and summation, both a bed of inherited culture (the deeper the better) and an alert, responsive – and critically responsive – audience (which in the case of teaching, may, with the right conditions, be provided by the class, the teacher, the school and the immediate community). The contemporary Socio-Linguistic School has also made an important and further contribution in emphasising the writer's need for an audience. In the next chapter we will consider further the place of the audience in the art-making process.

What do these principles of cultural continuity and critical community mean for English teaching? They point to three responsibilities. Firstly, there is the responsibility of the English teacher to initiate the child into the heritage of myth and literature, to provide the great but uncertain seed of impulse with a bed of culture, and, heeding the insights of the Progressives, to do this in intimate relationship to the child's age, needs and creative work. Secondly, there is the responsibility to slowly convert the class into a critical audience, at once receptive and discriminating; an audience, it must be added (extending the narrow Leavisian framework) not only for the traditional or contemporary writer 'out there', but also for the writer 'within', the child-writer, the adolescent-writer. Thirdly, and intimately related to the previous responsibilities, is the English teacher's task to develop an acute sensitivity to poetic language, to what D. H. Lawrence called 'art-speech'. Children should taste on their tongues the texture of words. In this, a delighting in words and a discriminating between them should become all but indistinguishable.

To return to Leavis, it can be seen how his great contribution to English lay in the critical and the collaborative domain. His strengths resided in: his awareness of the subtleties of language, his attention to the specific meanings of specific words in specific texts and contexts, in his appreciation of the vitality of tradition (including, particularly, that of the English novel and what he established as the organic line of English poetry), in his insistence on the existential relationship between literature and human life, in his teaching methods celebrating the 'third realm' *between* student and tutor, *between* critic and text, that process of collaboratively establishing tentative meaning in the act of teaching-and-learning. There were other strengths too: there was Leavis' courage to oppose what would seem to be the incurable pathologies of industrial culture; there was the refusal to compromise within or outside the university; there was the refusal to become academic; there was the implacable attack on all the metropolitan organs of our literary or would-be literary culture. His attack on prevailing orthodoxies and literary coteries isolated him severely and much of the criticism was marred by a note of megalomania and paranoia. Yet the work was necessary. It compelled attention as surely as it undermined comfort. It exposed the fifth-rate strutting as the first-rate. It provoked in the reader an engagement with his own impoverished yet euphoric age. Above all, it ripped away the pretences of colour-supplement thought and the facade of liberal publishing houses. Yet, as we shall see, there were severe limitations to Leavis' position, but before examining them, we must briefly make one more link between Leavis and the development of English in our schools.

As is well-known, the methods and principles of Leavis – and of many others who contributed to the influential *Scrutiny* – were taken into English teaching at the secondary level through the journal *The Use of English*, founded and edited by Denys Thompson (who had also in 1933 written with Leavis the first text-book on the mass-media *Culture and Environment* and who was later to be co-founder of the National Association for the Teaching of English). Through *The Use of English* and through the practice of English teachers who had studied literature at Downing College, the habits of critical evaluation of unseen passages, of introducing the best of contemporary literature (at that time, for example, D. H. Lawrence, T. S. Eliot and W. B. Yeats), of examining the vacuous rhetoric of advertising and mass-newspapers became widespread, particularly in the grammar schools. The seminal energies of the Cambridge School cannot be seriously denied. The work of David Holbrook (whose work was to dramatically extend the range of English), G. H. Bantock, Ian Robinson, Raymond Williams (who was to take much deeper, and make more complex, Leavis' sketchy analysis of mass-culture), Richard Hoggart, Fred Inglis, Frank Whitehead (who after Denys Thompson was to edit *The Use of English*), William Walsh, Boris Ford, the work of all these substantial writers, editors and critics had deep roots in the work of Leavis. It would be mere journalist patter to offer any summary of so many authors. I list them as only the crudest indication of the intellectual and critical power of the Cambridge School. Their contribution to a unified concept and detailed practice of English has been enormous.

What, then, were the flaws, the fatal inadequacies of conception in the Cambridge School? It was, firstly, limited in range. It tended to work intensively within English literature rather than to forge connections with other related traditions. Indeed, Leavis insisted on virtually defining the whole of healthy culture as literature; and this is not only nonsense, but dangerous nonsense, for it negates the exploration of human gesture – through all the other expressive, symbolic forms. Leavis' bias is here even narrower than Arnold's, and much narrower than Coleridge's. This contraction of range has had an unfortunate influence in our universities and schools, encouraging English to remain separate from the other expressive disciplines. English became a well-fortressed island rather than part of a unified archipelago. The defensive and monolithic attitude to literature served to keep English arrogantly isolated from the other complementary expressive arts. In the grammar schools many English departments became the centres of critical culture, but for all their excellence, there was a certain insularity of spirit, a failure to find the terms necessary for a full aesthetic education, a failure to discern the affinities between English and art.

Furthermore there was a marked tendency in the early Cambridge School to elevate the act of criticism above the act of creation. The very word *Scrutiny* unambiguously proclaimed what kind of activity is most esteemed. It is, I think, significant that in his teaching Leavis never asked his students to write in an imaginative capacity or even as a means to comprehend the nature of a particular form or genre. There was no recognition in his actual pedagogy of the way in which a student can gain from disciplined creative work. It is also pertinent to our critique that *Scrutiny* published a comparatively small amount of original poetry and that the only young poet the journal strongly promoted, Ronald Bottrall, has not, as his *Poems 1955–1973* testify, developed into a major voice. There was always the danger in the Cambridge School that criticism, cut off from the primary experience of artistic creation, would become dry, inturned, self-perpetuating: critics on critics on critics . . . And there was always the danger of original insight petrifying into dogma. Too often, Leavis' personal *credo* became simply the closed creed of lesser men (not women, it is interesting to observe). The circle instead of expanding, contracted. Did the master himself fall into the trap of wanting mirrors around him? Had he overlooked the wisdom in one of Nietzsche's aphorisms which claims that the good student has to go beyond the teacher, and that the teacher must urge him to do so? David Daiches has written:

> Leavis did not want admirers unless they admired him absolutely on his own terms. To say to him: 'I admire your criticism greatly; I go with you most of the way; but I disagree with you on some points and would like to argue with you about them' was as a rule received no better than denouncing him as an intolerant puritan . . . Agreement on major issues on the part of one who was not a 100 per cent disciple was unacceptable to him.[6]

Dialectically, we are driven back to the affirmations of the Progressives; back to the need for creative impulse, alert many-sidedness, authenticity of naive and stammering response, unfolding inner process. And, then, we grasp it! The Progressives and the Cambridge School represent two opposed but complementary sides of the human psyche, two sides ineradicably there and expressed throughout Western history in an unending variety of antitheses. In any reconstruction of English as art, both sides must be brought together, into an ever uneasy and ever creative co-existence. Tradition and innovation; criticism and creative impulse – these, are not antithetical concepts but, as we will show in the next chapter, complementary, dependent on each other and defined by each other. We need the firm arched bow and the flight of the arrow.

Historically it was the work of David Holbrook to attempt an act of synthesis, to bring together, as it were, 'the great tradition' and 'the education of the poetic spirit'. Coming out of the Cambridge School, studying under Leavis at Downing College, he could recognise the need for discrimination and critical awareness of the past, but, as a poet and novelist, he knew also the need to keep symbolism close to the creative springs of one's own existence, the deep need in all of us to give order to our confused and bewildering experience through the elaboration of phantasy and inward image. His indispensable books sought to fuse the best of literary criticism with the best of psychoanalysis. His writing sought to straddle two fiery traditions and drive them in a common direction. For over a decade *English for maturity* (1961) and *English for the Rejected* (1964) pointed a way forwards for English teaching. There is not space here to evaluate David Holbrook's seminal contribution to English but, without doubt, it has been seriously undervalued. From the perspective of this paper his work, while it did not adequately define English within the epistemic community of the arts and while it did not properly emphasise *the process of making*, of reworking, revising and shaping in children's writing, yet it did establish the concept of English as an expressive activity. With great eloquence, his early works celebrated English as imaginative, exploratory and aesthetic. But the direction towards the arts, which David Holbrook's books made possible again, became eclipsed by a further movement which, in our search for comprehensive principles, we must now examine.

V

The most influential force on English teaching, during the last fifteen years or so, has come from what I have already named as the Socio-Linguistic School, a school which has shown little appreciation or even knowledge of the Cambridge Movement or the earlier Progressive Movement. This contemporary movement has derived its inspiration less from literature or philosophy, than from linguistics and sociology. After the Newsom Report was published in 1963, the Sociological Research Unit was funded to analyse the relationship between language and social class. The project was directed by Basil Bernstein and came forward with the volatile notions of the restricted and elaborated codes. More generally, the nature of the work encouraged a new interest in *spoken* language, an interest revealed, for example, in Douglas Barnes' and James Britton's writings. A concern for speech had been missing in the previous traditions. The London Institute of Education with its sociological research into language and with its Postgraduate Certificate in Education course run by Harold Rosen, became both physically and symbolically one of the centres for the new English. The other centre was provided by the Nuffield Programme in Linguistics and English Teaching directed from 1964 to 1970 by M. A. K. Halliday. This project (having a more direct influence on English teaching than Bernstein's research) culminated in *Language in Use*, encouraging an analytical study of different forms of language, a text now found in many classrooms. It is not without significance that both these projects were given an official imprimatur by the Bullock Report, for in many ways the projects provide the ideological background to that massive document.

The great virtue of the Socio-Linguistic School was that it looked broadly at language and understood it as a formative energy of the mind seeking order and pattern. It saw language as crucial to the whole curriculum and gave a new significance to oracy, to the activity of speaking, to the daily personal making of meaning and order through informal discussion and immediate conversation. 'The spoken language in England', wrote Andrew Wilkinson, 'has been shamefully neglected. Oracy is central'. Unlike, for example, Arnold and Sampson in the literary tradition, the sociologists realised that there were many forms–idioms, registers, codes–of language, all, in their own context, appropriate and valuable. Halliday, on dialect and idiom, is eloquent:

> A speaker who is made ashamed of his own language habits suffers a basic injury as a human being: to make anyone, especially a child, feel so ashamed is as indefensible as to make him feel ashamed of the colour of his skin.[7]

Dialect, where it exists, it was argued, is not a corruption of English but a distinct expression of it, as valid, because it exists and is used, as any other form. In their respect for the variety of language, the Socio-Linguistic writers express a deeper conception of the complex nature of language than George Sampson and Matthew Arnold with their misconceived and imperialistic desire 'to set the standard of speech for the Empire'. It has been the distinct achievement of Bernstein, Barnes, Britton and Halliday to heighten *every* teacher's awareness of language by making him highly attentive to the different types of speech used by children in the classroom. The imperative 'Language across the curriculum' was the inevitable outcome.

The Sociolinguists' contribution to education has, in its own way, been as distinct as that of the earlier traditions of English. As with the traditions we have already described so with the Sociolinguists, they have provoked, shocked, and deeply challenged entrenched views. With their broad concern for 'language' and 'communication', they were able to cast a dazzling beam of light onto the mundane realities of so much teaching in this country. Against the reluctant acquisition of scattered information, which still passes for teaching and learning, the linguists asserted the primacy of process and the need for expressive language, that language through which each pupil personally makes sense of the facts and begins to grasp for himself the principles behind them. In massive attempts to clarify their own preoccupations with language and learning, the Sociolinguists hammered out fresh conceptual schemata which served to further expose the pedagogic confusion of our schools. At another level, their work constituted a critique of traditional positivist epistemology. The Sociolinguists were out to demonstrate that truth was not simply 'out there' to be imprinted on the passive mind of the child; but that it was made through individual attempts to actively formulate meaning. That, therefore, truth could only be found through the personal tussle to find words, symbols, representative forms. It followed that a school which did not allow the pupil space to formulate his own responses, thoughts, conceptions, destroyed the very premise on which any meaningful sense of education must stand. One particular merit of the Socio-Linguistic Movement has been its ability to keep principle and practice, abstract theory and tangible implication closely tethered. It has also had the courage to stand by its conclusions.

One schema elaborated by the Sociolinguists was the now too familiar 'transactional-expressive-poetic' division of language. Whatever objections may be brought against the classification (and the theory) it was richly productive and remains a useful tool. The following charts, for example, taken from *Writing and Learning across the Curriculum*, record, in a devastating manner, the amount of futile 'learning' which takes place in our secondary schools. In its abstract form it is as telling to our reason as Dicken's *Hard Times* is telling to our imagination, and it is telling the same truth; facts, facts, facts.

KINDS OF WRITING ACROSS THE SECONDARY CURRICULUM

	Year 1	Year 3	Year 5	Year 7
Transactional	54	57	62	84
Expressive	6	6	5	4
Poetic	17	23	24	7
Miscellaneous	23	14	9	5

Function by subject

	English	History	Geography	RE	Science
Transactional	34	88	88	57	92
Expressive	11	0	0	11	0
Poetic	39	2	0	12	0
Miscellaneous	26	10	12	20	0

It would take a whole volume or a month of seminars to draw out the full implications of these two charts. I reprint them here only as an example of the power of the linguist's schema to illuminate classroom practice and as an example of the kind of evidence marshalled to testify to the Sociolinguist's indictment of much teaching and learning. The diagram makes abundantly clear why a shift from literature to language took place, why it may even have been necessary and why the movement had to be, beneath the garbs of academic study and the classification of data, valuably subversive and engaged.

Yet the Socio-Linguistic School ultimately left the English teacher in a highly ambiguous position, an eagle stretched across the curriculum but without nest or offspring. All the research and all the writing revealed infinitely more about English as a medium (my second definition) than English as a discipline (my third definition). It contributed virtually nothing to the study of literature nor to the development of creative work, i.e. work, in their terms, moving from the expressive into the poetic category. In fact, although we shall move on to examine what happened to English, it is doubtful whether the Sociolinguists really believed in English as a unique discipline, with its own field and distinct pedagogy. Past formulations were cut away as if they had never been. Overnight, in the theory at least, English became either a sort of linguistics or a sort of social studies. Had there ever been other approaches? Had one asked such a tactless question, one might have heard the reply 'Leavis? Ah!—an elitist' or 'Holbrook? Marjorie Hourd? Lost in the (Bourgeois) vagaries of psycho-analysis!'

Two distinct approaches, emerged as possible answers to the fundamental question 'What is the discipline of English?' The first approach was to make English mean linguistics. We have already had occasion to mention *Language in Use*. The Bullock Report described this textbook as follows:

> The principle of the programme is to some extent like that of geographical and botanical field work, in that it involves studying specimens of language.

Language in Use attempted to turn English into a linguistic science, a cognitive, essentially neutral, introduction to verbal techniques. In the light of our argument so far such a substitution has to be sharply queried. Certainly such a text might be quite indispensable to the study of linguistics as an optional fifth form or sixth form course. What it cannot be is an adequate substitute for the discipline of English as it has built up over the last eighty years, with its commitment to the cultural heritage and to the emotional development of the individual through the agency of the creative word. Linguistics is a specialised analytical study of language in all its variety; English as a discipline tends to concentrate on one specific form of language: language charged with feeling and personality, the language of the individual (whether pupil or mature writer) moved by the power of feeling or compelled by the unifying force of imagination. As I will show in chapter 3, English is practical and expressive, linguistics is theoretical and scientific. The disciplines have language in common, but their methods and aims are, for most of the time, quite different.

Another way of expressing our opposition to Linguistics in this specific context is to say that English is centrally concerned with the making and appreciation of literature. Yet literature, in many of the arguments for linguistics, became reduced to being little more than just another manifestation of language, a manifestation that was even dying out, that was, perhaps, in no way essential to the functioning of materialist civilization. Peter Doughty, in characteristic vein, declared that the new English teacher should be committed to 'language in all its complexity and variety and *not merely the highly idiosyncratic form of literature*'. The highly idiosyncratic form of Homer, Shakespeare and D. H. Lawrence! Halliday, in the same light or, more truly, in the same darkness, insisted that the true discipline for the English teacher was no longer literature – that idiosyncratic version of language destined to die out in the TV metropolis – but linguistics. It was as if F. R. Leavis and David Holbrook and countless others had never lifted their pens. Earlier traditions of English teaching had been, with alarming efficiency, simply erased. In the numb space buzzed the small insects 'communications', 'skills', 'strategies', 'language operates', the drone of a new technicism. Curiously, as the word 'communication' fell like lead from the lips of a thousand teachers, so there seemed less and less to say. What had been overlooked in the pathological obsession for communications was the elusive underground of the psyche, those preconceptual sources of latent formulation locked in the emergent impulses of the body and the unconscious. Only by maintaining contact with these deeper pre-verbal energies can language itself remain resonant, charged, rich, strange, compelling and worthwhile. Creativity exists prior to words. And words, if they are to have the power of authentic utterance, must return constantly to their non-verbal origins, back to the creative impulse. The rejection of psycho-analysis had, indeed, been premature. Without any sense of depth or inner mystery, 'communication' was destined to become confined to surfaces, growing ever thinner and ever more transparent until there was nothing left to say, except words.

The second approach has been to take English in the direction of social studies, into the explicit and continuous discussion (theoretically 'neutral', although in fact often slanted ideologically to the Left) of social and moral issues. The themes were generally presented through literary, and not so literary, extracts. The most well known example of this approach was Lawrence Stenhouse's *Humanities Project* with its 'relevant' material (on the family, on war, etc.) with its insistence on the teacher as 'neutral chairman' and its goal of 'tolerance'. There was nothing particularly new in the *Humanities Project*. As early as 1963 in the textbook *Reflections* there had been a marked shift in English towards the discussion of social issues through the reading of extracts from a largely contemporary literature. At the time (in the early sixties) the approach seemed convincing and, without doubt, it encouraged some excellent work in the classroom, particularly in the socially-mixed classrooms of the new comprehensives. But after a decade or so, with the publication of innumerable anthologies parading the nightmares of pollution, abortion, unemployment, racial segregation, teacher and parent cruelty, strikes, women's liberation, prostitution, homosexuality, alcoholism, drug addiction, social exploitation, children's rights, nuclear war, suicide and the futility of the educational system, the approach became –how shall we say it? – sordidly nihilistic.

From the point of view of this book however, a more important objection has to be recorded about this kind of work being done under the umbrella of English for its proper epistemological roots lie not in English but in sociology and ethics. If literature is employed solely to spark off a discussion of 'issues', moving ever away from the metaphor to the abstraction, then imaginative texts are being roughly abused. They are not being conveyed, but betrayed. There is little doubt in my mind that during the last fifteen years, under the influence of the Socio-Linguistic School, much literature has been betrayed in our classroom, twisted from high imaginative art into quick ideological stimulus. The logical direction of such a method has, in many of our schools, taken English into common humanities courses. In such an alliance English tends to lose that unique mode of imaginative and emotional indwelling in literature, that response where one is not irritably seeking out social issues for rational debate, but, rather, trying to identify and grow with newly felt emergent experience. We politicize literature at the cost of authenticity. Again, it is a matter of renewing faith in forces which transcend the merely given, of allowing art its own underground logic and, yes, its own kind of poetic 'praxis'.

One further and intimately related objection must be recorded. There is, among the Sociolinguists I have rather brutally caged together, a certain predilection to convert educational disciplines into ideological weapons. In the writing of Harold Rosen, Labov and Chris Searle we cannot but discern a compulsive identification of English with the oppressed members of our society – with the immigrants, the unemployed, the proletariat – which, while it draws heavily on our desires for social justice, yet in an educational context becomes out of place and dangerously exclusive. In its worst forms it is philistine, sentimental and highly destructive. It would dismiss the whole of English literature as bourgeois culture and, without any qualification or unease, erect the razamatazz of the slum-street into the only form of authentic existence. Analysing the position of Chris Searle, Sonia Courtnadge has written:

> Although Searle criticises middle-class society as one which thrives on divisions, I would argue what he is doing is equally divisive. The approach is one which seeks to insulate the child within his own environment and 'class', for, in order to achieve working class solidarity, the pupils are urged to eschew all 'middle class' language and literature and 'to see his own life in terms of his immediate surroundings, his own world'. He will gain his knowledge from his neighbours and environment, not from a different consciousness at school.[10]

At its best, education must spring from a universality of principle; it must strive to be comprehensive rather than partial and should seek to feed that deep human impulse for transcendence. It must avoid bolstering all comfortable enclosing presuppositions, inertly inherited; it does not matter where the presuppositions come from, from the country house, from the suburban semi-detached or the slum-dwelling. Education is a fearless enquiry into human meaning and an energy for diverse authentic growth; it is not a pre-selected political struggle. It is an act of making whose outcome cannot be told until the last poem is written and the last theory hypothesised. Perhaps the Sociolinguists have been guilty of trying to close the very process which they have worked so diligently to make open? And this, as is so often the case, with the best of political intentions, the finest of moral convictions.

I have implied that the concept of English as a medium across the curriculum has been the major contribution of the Sociolinguists. I wish to draw this element in particular from the work of the Institute and the Bullock Report because it provides one of the necessary conditions for the autonomy of English as a literary-expressive discipline. But here, at least, we find a continuity. In 1975 James Britton in introducing *Writing and Learning across the Curriculum* had written:

> One of the most far-reaching changes in education envisaged by the Bullock Committee is to be found in its recommendation that all teachers should seek to foster learning in their particular areas by taking responsibility for the language development of their students in that area.[11]

'Far-reaching' it no doubt was. And yet in 1920, fifty-five years before in *English for the English* George Sampson had anticipated the same principle:

> . . . no teachers, whether of sciences, or languages or mathematics, or history or geography must be allowed to evade their own heavy responsibilities. They must not say 'our business is to teach science or mathematics or French, not English'. That is the great fallacy of 'subject teaching'. It is very definitely their business to teach English; and their failure to recognise it as their business is a cause of the evil they deplore. In a sense the function of history, geography, science and so forth in school is to provide material for the teaching of English. The specialist teacher defeats his own purpose precisely to the extent to which he neglects the language of his pupils.[12]

In the notion of language across the curriculum, we find a further tenet necessary for the reconstruction of English as art. If all teachers are rightfully concerned with the development of language as it relates to their own particular subject then English as a discipline is released to occupy its own place in the curriculum. Ironically, what that place is has been badly obscured by those very arguments which engendered the principle. But in this analysis we have grown accustomed to the necessary partiality of evolving ideas; to one truth blotting out another to establish itself and then in establishing itself to reveal its inadequacies. Ideas and movements grow dialectically and require, in turn, a dialectical approach. What is omitted is as crucial as what is asserted.

What we begin to see emerging out of the traditions is yet a further shape to English, which incorporates the best of the past, and yet remains new in its more comprehensive pattern and still awaits its full formation, its necessary practice. Before turning to this vital redefinition of English as art, it is, unfortunately, necessary to make one further critique of a tradition (it does not deserve the gravity of that concept) which can still be seen to underlie the teaching of English. It is the simple enduring notion that English consists essentially of prescriptive grammar, closed comprehension and set composition.

VI

In the invaluable study *The Teaching of English in Schools* David Shayer wrote:

> What must disturb anyone who looks into the history of the subject in this country is the extent to which practices have been established for reasons often only tenuously connected with well thought out English theory and have then assumed a permanence generation after generation which is seemingly unshakeable.[13]

Certainly, this is the case with that still largely unshaken trinity of English teaching: grammar, comprehension and composition. The reasons for their existence have always been tenuous in nature, deriving either from demands made by other disciplines in the curriculum or from prejudices and misconceptions operating from within. I want here to briefly scrutinize, in turn, each member of the trinity. First, grammar. Then, comprehension. And, finally, composition.

Even though the 'O' Level Language Paper has for some time set no questions on grammar, a number of teachers still regard it as an essential part of English. Yet all the major reports have doubted or denied the value of an abstract and prescriptive grammar. As early as 1921 the Newbolt Report quoted with respect P. B. Ballard who put the negative case quite unequivocally:

> I have convinced myself by an extensive inquiry that in the elementary school formal grammar:
> *(a)* fails to provide a general mental training;
> *(b)* does not enable the teachers to eradicate solicisms;
> *(c)* does not aid in composition;
> *(d)* takes up time, which could be more profitably devoted to the study of literature.[14]

Although quoting Ballard sympathetically the Newbolt Report, nevertheless, equivocated. It decided, in a considerable state of confusion, that knowledge of grammar was essential because the teaching of foreign languages required it! Even George Sampson in his seminal book *English for the English*, while asserting that the child would get little help in his writing or speech from the study of grammar, concurred with the conclusion of the Newbolt Report. Practice once established withers slowly. Prescriptive grammar still casts its ominous shadow over many English departments and over language work in many primary schools. Yet it would seem from 1921 onwards the practice was justified by quite extraneous arguments, arguments which had nothing to do with mother-tongue English or with English as a discipline.

For over two decades official reports on English struggled to free English from the abstract and mechanical approaches fostered by prescriptive grammar. The HMSO Report *The Examining of English Language* published in 1964 complained of exercises 'based on traditionally prescribed rules of grammar which have been artifically imposed upon the language'. And continued: 'They have had little relevance to usage at any past time and they have even less to contemporary usage'. In 1975 the Bullock Report in its comment on grammar claimed:

> Such a prescriptive view of language was based on a comparison with classical Latin, and it also mistakenly assumed an unchanging quality in both grammatical rules and word meaning in English.[15]

The Report then referred to an experimental study in which one class in each of five schools was taught grammar in a formal manner for over two years. During the same period of time another corresponding class in each school was given no grammar lessons. These classes were instead given plenty of writing practice based on an inductive approach to usage. At the end of the period, both groups were given a writing test and a grammar test. In the writing test those classes which had worked pragmatically scored significantly higher scores than those which had worked through a formal grammar approach. Furthermore, there was no significant correlation between high scores in the grammar test and ability in writing. The Bullock Report concluded: 'What has been shown is that the teaching of traditional analytical grammar does not appear to improve performance in writing'. It is a conclusion which many of us, who studied grammar at school and who still struggle to write, can personally verify. In general, it can be said that just as we learn to swim by swimming, by making the necessary actions in the element of water and not by studying the detailed movements of our body muscles, so we learn to *speak by speaking, to write by writing*. There is no causal connection between a technical knowledge of a language and the ability to use it. Thus as English teachers we can discard neurotic anxieties about traditional grammar. Furthermore, we can legitimately ask those teaching second languages to introduce the concepts necessary for their own work. As English teachers, it is simply not our task.

If traditional grammar, with its logical patterns deriving from Latin rather than English, has been officially discredited, the exercise known as comprehension has survived for decades virtually unscathed. In 1921 the Newbolt Committee recommended that exercises in comprehension should form the only compulsory element in an examination of the English language. Nearly fifty years later, comprehension retains its eminent position both in the examination system and in the teaching of English, at least in the upper part of the secondary school. But is comprehension an exercise which has only tenuous justification, an exercise which has continued out of inertia or even perhaps an unconscious anxiety as to what to put in its place? Certainly, as it exists at the moment, it is a tedious and futile affair. When, in life, do we perform an act resembling the school comprehension exercise? Probably never.

What does 'doing' a piece of comprehension amount to? The pupils are asked to respond quite impersonally to a dislocated passage in terms of a sequence of pre-set questions. A critic recently referred to these random passages, gathered in volume after volume of Comprehension Exercises for 'O' Level, as 'literary flotsam left stranded on the exam beach'. The students are expected to demonstrate their literal understanding of various isolated parts of an already isolated extract of prose. When that has been done, the exercise is complete. As the Bullock Report pointed out there is little reason to suppose that the student transfers what he has learnt to other passages which come his way. And there is no reason why he should. The comprehension exercise, like the grammar which used often to accompany it, has become nothing more than a soulless routine, given a spurious status simply because of its disproportionate place in the English language examination papers.

If Comprehension is to have any value it should demand a greater response and penetration of the passage in question. It should include much more than the mere mechanical understanding of the disconnected parts. Most important of all, such work should ensure that the pupils themselves generate pertinent questions in response to what they have read. Such an ability to generate questions is a crucial part of education, an inveterate tendencey of the educated mind. (We do well to remember that propaganda and advertisements have no open-ended questions printed beneath.) In education, this art of generating articulate questions in response to given statements or judgements cannot be over-estimated. Any worthwhile Comprehension, then should include:

(*a*) personal and intelligent evaluation of the passage
(*b*) the generating in the pupil of counter-argument, alternative evidence, excluded materials, etc.
(*c*) a placing of the passage in terms of its style.

More formally, we could, depending on the passage – and I am assuming here an argumentative passage – divide the tasks into the following categories:

QUESTIONS DERIVING FROM CONTEXT
Why was the passage written? i.e. What would seem to be the motives for writing it?
Who is it addressed to? How can you tell?
Where, would you say, has it been taken from? How do you know?

QUESTIONS ABOUT STYLE
How does the writer present his case?
What are the distinguishing marks of the writing?

QUESTIONS TESTING PUPILS' UNDERSTANDING
What is the conclusion of the author?
What are the main arguments presented?

QUESTIONS TESTING PUPILS' EVALUATION
What other arguments might the author have used?
What arguments might be developed against it?
To what extent, do you agree with the argument?

QUESTIONS TESTING PUPILS' POWER OF COMMUNICATION
Write a short letter to the local paper explaining briefly the author's position.
Write to a friend describing your response to the passage.

All this work could be done, just as effectively, orally. What one is seeking to establish in such work is *an alert play of mind over what is read*, an ability not only to understand literal meanings but an ability to recreate the content of the passage and, not least, the ability to tussle with it intellectually. One is promoting in the pupil the habit of critical reading.

The question arises: to what extent is the comprehension exercise, even in its superior shape, an integral part of English? At points, it must be – for the process of evaluation is essential to the reading of literature and to the discussion of children's imaginative work in writing and in drama. At the same time, the habit of critical reading, particularly where it is concerned with rational argument and the scrupulous weighing up of diverse evidence, is crucial to both the humanities and the sciences. Comprehension, in brief, in the extended form which I have suggested, should be assumed as an essential aspect of good pedagogy.

What were we doing last week?
Why did we reach that conclusion?
What other conclusions were suggested?
Why were they discarded?
Were we right to discard them?
Who can think of another possible explanation?
What are the weakness of this new theory?
When, then, does a scientist accept a theory as reliable?

One would have thought such questions in comprehension and evaluation would have accompanied the teaching of science at any level. Questions, couched to develop understanding, scepticism, mental agility, should teem through the bloodstream of the humanities and sciences. Why, then, when the habit is vital to most disciplines, should English teachers be specifically concerned with imparting the techniques of comprehension?

In its rather sober discussion of the place of comprehension, the Bullock Report claimed:

> It must be developed in a range of contexts where it is put to a practical purpose and that means in the various subjects of the curriculum. The techniques themselves might be learnt in the English lesson, but the kind of co-operation we envisage should ensure that the subject teacher followed this up with practical application.[16]

Wisely, the comprehension exercise is dissolved back into the curriculum, an essential element for which all teachers are responsible. As for the techniques, the Bullock Report, desperately holding onto the saddle after the horse has bolted, suggests these *might* be learnt in the English lesson. But techniques, in fact, are always best studied in living contexts. The historian, the geographer, the scientist, teaches the method of summary as it relates to his discipline. The skills are taken back into the specific contexts which call them forth. In this way the English teacher discovers a new space for the intrinsic demands and meanings of his discipline. Through language across the curriculum, English as a discipline is freed to find its own intrinsic shape as an arts discipline.

Let us now turn to the last member of the conventional trinity, composition. The writing of a miniature essay has been standard procedure in English teaching from before 1900 and would seem to derive from the nineteenth century literary milieu where established authors wrote 'occasional pieces', in a leisurely if rather inflated style, for thriving journals. At some point, in the back of some unknown examiner's mind, there must have been the notion that good prose writing came in the form of witty, entertaining essays, perhaps, in the manner of a Charles Lamb or a Thomas Macaulay. It is, I think, relevant to observe that Newbolt, Chairman of the 1921 report on English, himself edited just such a selection of occasional literary pieces. His *Essays and Essayists*, a collection not to be simply dismissed, includes such titles as 'My books', (Leigh Hunt), 'The ideal house' (R.L. Stevenson), 'Gifts' (Mary Coleridge), 'July' (Mrs Meynell), 'Old China' (Charles Lamb) and 'On national prejudices' (Oliver Goldsmith). The titles themselves sound, in retrospect, like 'O' Level Composition titles. At the beginning of the century, such literary, refined essays were seen as providing ideal models and pupils were expected to reproduce them. Such exercises in literary extravagance called forth further superfluities from thousands of school children.

Of course, the compositions set by examiners have been criticized. The 1964 report on *The Examining of English Language* aptly called the artificial essays encouraged by the quaint titles as 'exercises in belles-lettrism' and claimed that they easily led to 'an insincere kind of writing' both derivative and pretentious. But as with comprehension, so with composition, the ill-conceived forms of the past, once established, continue to determine current practice. Here, for example is part one of a recent 'O' level examination paper with its grim prefatory warnings:

> Remember to pay attention all through the paper to spelling, punctuation, and the construction of sentences.

PART I

Write a composition on *one* of the following subjects. You should cover about two sides of the writing paper and *not more than three*.

Either, (*a*) On being well dressed.

Or,   (*b*) You have two friends who are treated quite differently by their parents. Margaret has to be in at night by 10 o'clock, and up in the morning to help her mother. No television is allowed before homework is done. When she goes out, parents must know where and with whom. She has regular pocket money. Philip, on the other hand, goes out and comes in when he likes, and no questions are ever asked. At home he arranges his life according to his own ideas. Often at weekends he has a good 'lie in'. He asks for what money he wants, and usually gets it.
    What do you think of these two different ways of bringing up children?

Or,   (*c*) The trap.

Or,   (*d*) On being a rebel – or a conformist.

Or,   (*e*) Tinkering with engines.

Or,   (*f*) Trying new recipes.[17]

Notice the artificiality of many of the titles, ('On being well dressed', 'Tinkering with engines', 'Trying new recipes') the constraints set by time (one hour!), and the explicit 'remember to pay attention all through the paper to spelling, punctuation and the construction of sentences'. What are the examiners looking for? A breezy acquaintance with the universe? An ability to insert full stops? The power to have finished at the stroke of the clock? Yes, probably all of these. And, perhaps, little else.

Why has the composition survived? I have said it has survived through inertia and fear. But there are other reasons. The following excerpt is taken from a publisher's blurb for yet another book of English essay exercises:

> The essay is a major feature of all English Language examinations and therefore deserves a good share of classroom attention and practice. It is also fair to claim that time given to learning how to write English language essays will bring benefit to other school subjects and provide a sound base for writing papers, reports and business letters in later life.[18]

The blurb offers three further 'reasons' for the essay. Firstly, it exists on the examination. Secondly, it is required by other disciplines. Thirdly, it will be useful in industrial society later. Such arguments are frequently used to justify conventional English. Yet because an exercise exists on the examination, it does not follow it is valuable practice; because other subjects require essay-writing does not prove that it should be an intrinsic concern of English as a discipline. Likewise with industry. If industry requires certain skills it in no way logically follows that education should work to provide them. The thinking behind 'O' Level practice, in brief, is spurious. Such thinking demonstrates just how tenuous reasons can be for the time-honoured pursuits of the English teacher. And, as we have seen, these pursuits, once established, assume a permanence generation after generation 'seemingly unshakeable'.

What is so inadequate and false about the syllabus virtually imposed on English teachers by the GCE 'O' level language papers? I would say that the syllabus, made up of comprehension and composition, is largely unnecessary because these activities should be developed extensively elsewhere in the curriculum. For the art of collecting and reformulating information, the power to summarize, the ability to connect various points and to make out of them rational totalities, the capacity to develop a point of view with regard to the object one is examining, the powers, in brief, to read and write both critically and intelligently are essential not only to all the humanities but to the sciences as well. As early as 1921 the Newbolt Report pointed out 'every teacher is a teacher of English because every teacher is a teacher in English'. All academic disciplines, taught well, must develop in the young the skills of reading (like skimming, scanning, use of an index, comprehension and evaluation) and the skills of writing (note-taking, ability to organize notes into arguments, ability to organize arguments into essays). These are not extraneous items for the English department alone to develop. They are intrinsic to the process of thinking effectively whether as an historian, as a sociologist, as a biologist or as a scientist. It would not seem disproportionate to claim that the humanites and the sciences have looked, rather pathetically, to English departments for total support in matters of language, through a pedagogic laziness, through lack of awareness and unreflecting habit. The intelligent diffusion of the concepts; language across the curriculum, reading across the curriculum, writing across the curriculum, speaking across the curriculum, composition across the curriculum, comprehension across the curriculum, will radically alter the traditional pattern. In one of its principal recommendations the Bullock Report requested that:

> Each school should have an organized policy for language across the curriculum, establishing every teacher's involvement in language and reading throughout the years of schooling.[19]

As we have already argued such a policy provides the condition for the release of English. It lifts off the imposed manacles. It leaves English as a discipline free to assert its own nature, its existential, creative and imaginative propensities, its commitment to literature and myth, to metaphor and prophecy, its closeness to all the arts, its fundamental expressive and aesthetic nature.

VII

The analysis in this chapter has been highly condensed and highly schematic (doing no justice to any of the individuals I have either quoted or listed). As I said at the outset my account is not a neutral one, not a historian's account, not an account for posterity. Rather it is an analysis provoked by a feeling of disquiet about the existing state of English, since, say, the time of the 'Bullock' report. Certainly by the beginning of the eighties I felt that English had become impossibly diffuse in its interests, too eclectic in its approaches and too narrowly political in many of its formulations. At the same time, there was the miserable knowledge that in many classrooms across the country there had been an appalling reversion to habits which had been condemned as early as 1920, those old habits, for example, of grammatical dissection and the filling in of blanks inserted into, otherwise impeccably dull, sentences. English departments, quite simply, had lost direction and faced a dismal future in which they might cease to exist except as 'communications' or as 'skills laboratories' serving the other established disciplines. Above all, as I said in my introduction, English had neglected the aesthetic realm, leaving the curriculum pathologically biased towards the cognitive.

Some of the most convincing work on English as a discipline during the last decade has been the Schools Council project on the arts, in Robert Witkin's *The intelligence of feeling*, and in Malcolm Ross' *The Arts and the Adolescent* and *The Creative Arts*. These publications, I believe, struggle to provide a conceptual framework in which English, as an expressive discipline, could begin to thrive. To their work, we should bring, experimentally, the principles I have extracted from the three traditions of English teaching:

From the Progressives, the emphasis on impulse and the innate tendency towards individuation.

From the Cambridge School, the emphasis on tradition, discrimination and critical audience.

From the Sociolinguists the emphasis on process and the clarifying principle of 'Language across the Curriculum'.

As we shall see the implications of such a reconstruction of English could be quite revolutionary. For the first time in this country English would be drawn into the circle of the other, much neglected, expressive disciplines. New forms of collaboration would emerge from this encounter (the skilled printing and illustrating of prose and poetry, the setting of original songs to music, common Arts Festivals in the schools, the dramatic improvision of myth and fable). Such collaborations and joint productions would encourage vigorous thinking about the nature of creativity and, perhaps, begin to illuminate that dark area we designate 'affective' – and then forget – in our academic books on education. And, almost of necessity, such awareness would lead to an arts programme which would demand what it has never had in state education, a fitting share of the curriculum, i.e. about one third rather than, as at present, one tenth of the whole.

The arts form one indispensable symbolic form for the integration of experience. If in this country we are to talk of a core curriculum then we must include, without ambiguity or hesitation, the arts. What we now need to hear on the lips of teachers and parents is not so much the cry 'English (as a medium) across the curriculum' although that is still necessary. What is more urgent is the cry 'English (as a discipline) within the arts' and, finally, 'The arts within a total curriculum'.

But how are we to begin to move forward in the establishment of English as a literary-expressive discipline within the arts? We need, I think, to understand the common nature of the creative process as it manifests itself in all the arts. We need a common language for art-making. We need to bring the truths of the three traditions I have analysed to bear upon the experience of art-making and in doing so to go beyond them. In the next chapter this is exactly what I propose to do. My first concern is not with English as such but with English as it fits into the broader category of the arts, with the whole business of giving tangible form to the innumerable invisible currents of our experience, the business of expressive symbol-making. When I have had a preliminary stab at demarcating the common ground I will return in chapter 3 to describe the unique nature of English as a literary-expressive discipline.

2

The Pattern of Art-Making

I

Creative impulse, critical evaluation, cultural heritage, process before product, the need for a critical audience. With the rough tools of dialectical analysis these are some of the necessary concepts we have managed to extract from the three main traditions in English teaching. But there must be no misunderstanding. Our intention is not merely to melt down the three schools and cunningly shape them into one. A school of thought, a mode of enquiry, a way of working comes into existence at a certain time partly in response to the needs of the time, partly as the necessary outcome of an original and percipient thinker. A school is made out of two forces, historical need and intellectual vision. It is no accident that the Cambridge School of English, with its emphasis on selection, discrimination and cultivated minorities, coincided with the split of education into grammar and secondary schools and that the Socio-Linguistic School coincided with the era of the Comprehensive school. These highly complex patterns of inter-relationship – barely hinted at in the above examples, – are there to be discerned and are given representation by the sensitive sociologist and one kind of novelist. Ideas and social process are so closely intermingled, so reciprocally entangled, that it is impossible to say that one is unambiguously the causal agent of the other. What would seem certain is that any school making deep inroads into the consciousness of its age does so because it corresponds to deep personal and social needs. The philosophy is called forth by the manifest confusions and latent aspirations of the times which it seeks to give a new order to, an explication meeting the existential needs. The London Institute's work on English as language and communication is intimately related to the actual phenomena in London schools, all those different languages exploding inside the mono-linguistic classroom, all that cultural diversity, represented by innumerable immigrants, expanding in institutions traditionally confined not even to one language but to one type of discourse within that language. Theory as developed by a school of thought exists in some sort of dynamic relationship to the actual mess of living. Seminal texts are inevitably written in historical contexts which, in part, draw them forth.

In our analysis of the English traditions it was not our business to describe the criss-crossings of text and context, though they do have a bearing on our major theme, the reconstitution of English as art. For there is no way in which an alternative version of English can be created through, as it were, a cerebral amalgamation of nicely balancing parts. The elements I have selected *are* important but they need tethering to a greater vivifying principle. The concepts I have extracted have to be placed in a new matrix, to be given there a new kind of meaning, a further ambiance. As I have indicated, I believe that this generative principle is: English, not as a literary-critical discipline, but as a literary-expressive discipline within the wider epistemic community of the arts. The new principle, stresses the expressive act, both in original creation and in the re-creation, through performance, of the work of others. *The expressive act* – and the kinds of discipline which facilitate it – this is the unifying concern of English redefined within the arts. And, as in this chapter we begin to elaborate upon the common nature of the expressive act as it is manifested in all the arts, so we will find our received notions of 'impulse' and 'process', of 'inherited culture' and 'attentive audience' entering into the discourse but often with a subtle though decisive shift in meaning. The new context will re-define our understanding of what these terms mean. Thus in English practised as an expressive discipline, 'criticism' will not have quite the same import as given by the Cambridge School, or 'creativity' the same import as it had for the Progressives or 'process' for the Socio-Linguists. Furthermore, if English takes the road into the arts I am advocating, there would be a further enriching influx of concepts, methods, habits of doing and saying and evaluating coming from all the other arts. The results of such an influx cannot be determined in advance, but that it would have an energising and liberating force can hardly be doubted.

But what is the broad social context which makes this argument for English within the arts and the arts within a total curriculum, urgent and compelling? I would say it was the deep desire, so suppressed by contemporary society, for a sense of personal and communal identity. The art-making process is pre-eminently concerned with the development of consciousness through the creation and recreation of symbolism within a critical and responsive community. The quest for personal meaning lies at the centre of human existence. Yet when we inspect the society about us we find so little space for this ineradicable need. We find an objective materialism which has lost connection with the deep needs of the psyche, which organizes without reference to human meaning and quantifies without reference to human qualities. We find every-where human life disconnected from its sources and subservient to the two great impersonal forces of Production and Consumption. I have described in *Proposal for a New College* and in *The Black Rainbow* the stark conditions our society provides for inward growth. This is not the place to elaborate on those arguments. It must suffice to say that the great unspoken questions of our time relate to identity and to community, the need to be and the need to belong. I believe that the arts, above all other disciplines, directly address these needs and provide the creative means to answering them. This text is written within such a social context where the personal desire for meaning and community is constantly suppressed or thwarted or diverted by an uneasy and highly precarious industrial society.

II

The common ground of the art-making process in all the Arts is still relatively unexplored, still largely uncharted. One of the distinct merits of Robert Witkin's work *The Intelligence of Feeling* is that it sought to provide the elements of a comprehensive language for art teachers (in which term he perceptively included English teachers). While much of his terminology lacks eloquence, many of Witkin's distinctions are of undoubted importance and much of my own argument follows in the wake of his book and the subsequent uneven symposium by Malcolm Ross, *The Creative Arts*. Part of the value of Witkin's contribution to arts teaching lies in the fact that he does not only offer a critique of current practice, he also offers an alternative to it. The work is pioneering and a decade ahead of its time. Yet it is also severely flawed by its own style of presentation. The language of the book is invariably alien to the activities it purports to describe. Many of Witkin's concepts would seem to derive from academic psychology and bear with them the offensive and inexpungable connotations of mechanism. The poisoned terminology pollutes his own keen insights. The war being fought is that between emergent meaning and outworn terminology and the battleground is the first chapter of *The intelligence of feeling*. For all its occasional epigrammatic brilliance – where the insights flash forth across the murk of jargon – it is all but unreadable. And the failure of that first chapter hints at a problem which confronts all who would follow. What kind of language is appropriate to describe art-making? It must be, I feel, a language which complements what it delineates. It must be accurate, yes. But, surely, it must also be, wherever possible, resonant, lyrically sharp, eloquently unfolded. It must be a language with a human face; a language which responsive teachers, without artificiality, can use, take into their practice, try out, and adapt or discard according to their experience. We must resist a language which in its very feel denies the meaning of its subject. Thus when Witkin writes:

> If the price of finding oneself in the world is that of losing the world in oneself, then the price is more than anyone can afford.[20]

We sense an arresting eloquence of formulation, conveying profound human insight. But when a few pages later he proclaims:

> The projection of a behavioural medium through its object medium is therefore the projection of the past of behaviour in the present of the object medium, and the projection of an object medium through its behavioural medium is the project of the past of the object in the present of the behavioural medium.[21]

We have to point out that such a language, impossibly cumbersome, unnecessarily abstract, cannot catch the subtle movement of art-making. It obscures more than it reveals; reduces more than it opens out.

There are innumerable ways of coming to the arts. My way is determined by my focus; the expressive and communicative nature of art-making in the context of education. My aim, like Witkin's, is to conceptually delineate the various stages in the creation of art and to make explicit its educational value. I am out to provide a schema which illuminates the creative process in the arts, and which thereby enlightens classroom practice. I am out to reveal the pattern – the distinct paradigm – which characterises the expressive disciplines making them a single epistemic community. As Witkin and Malcolm Ross have demonstrated, the lack of such a language in our schools is in itself symptomatic of the confusion and fragmentation which prevails. Yet without a language, delineating the common rhythm and common purposes of art-making, there can be no general coherence in the arts – only further versions of the barely existing ad-hoc arts-jumble we have had in our schools for the best part of a century. It is to these common rhythms and common purposes that I now wish to turn.

III

It is not my aim to provide a comprehensive theory of the origins of art but any such theory would have to consider the connection between impulse and expressive symbol. In our nocturnal dreams and involuntary day-time phantasies we encounter the strange, elusive conversion of impulse into image and dramatic narrative. It is important to note that we do not learn how to dream or how to have phantasies. They are not abilities socially acquired, not events which have been nurtured by society. Rather, image-making would seem to be an innate activity of the psyche and the images would seem to represent diverse impulses within the psyche and soma, impulses released by the social and natural world outside as much as by the archetypal world within. We thus discover in the psyche itself an inherent creativity and a kind of 'natural' art, a symbolic life within our biological nature.

One of the functions of the art-maker is to enter into a creative relationship with this flow of impulse and its spume of imagery. By entering into such a relationship he brings a further shaping creativity to the spontaneous creativity of his own nature. The art-maker elaborates, refines and deepens the spontaneous movement of psyche towards imagery and reflection. His aim is to convert the hidden elusive art of his own being into the visible and enduring art of culture. He gives subjectivity an objective representation so that he can come *to know* his own experience. The art-maker, always working within his own historic culture and with the tools and traditions made available by that culture, is thus an agent in the promotion of consciousness, both his own and that of his audience who recognize in his work the hidden forms of human experience taken to fulfilment.

This is only one way of looking at art-making and, as I will show later, it needs anchoring more firmly into the ground of history and society (for even our bodies participate in history and society and are never pure zoological forces). Yet it has the merit of making art both a natural and an epistemological affair. Art is very close to the daily rhythms of human existence, the beat of the blood as it courses through the body, the constant inhaling and exhaling of breath, the habitual conversion of impulse into imagery, the busy life of all the senses. Yet it is also epistemological because in seeking to create formal patterns from the actual patterns of life, it comes to symbolize the possible meanings of human experience. Expressed like this, the educational significance of art becomes clear: art is to do with self-knowledge, the integration of impulse into consciousness, the conversion of sensation into meaning. As science, seen as a symbolic form, is concerned with a potential knowing of the outer universe through experimental and deductive reasoning; so the arts are concerned with a positive knowing of emotion, feeling and instinct through the making and sympathetic consideration of expressive forms. Both are concerned with knowledge through the means of symbolic creation. Both are epistemic communities. In both there is an irreducible cognitive dimension.

To understand this cognitive aspect we have to understand the movement from impulse to symbol to understanding. The process in art is, as we have stated, very close to ordinary processes in life. We constantly talk about our experiences in an attempt to know them from within. The more powerful the experience, the more we need to talk; or to dream or to phantasize. Let me give two examples of this process: one concerning the integration of intense feelings of anxiety, the other concerning feelings of shame.

The first example concerns one of my students, Chris King. The following account is a description taken from his journal of the way in which during his teaching practice in a Sussex comprehensive school Chris had to struggle to come to terms with an overwhelming sense of anxiety:

> During the last year, probably the most intense concern I have had, has been to face the anxieties of becoming an authority figure in front of twenty to thirty kids, several of whom were very reluctant to accept my attempts to negotiate order. For a couple of months in particular I found it very difficult to go for very long without this sense of anxiety gnawing away at me, often as though inside my stomach, and coming to dominate my thoughts. My seemingly endless attempts to rationally think through the situation rarely brought more than a fleeting sense of control. It seemed that such thoughts failed to even touch the depth of my feelings of anxiety which had a number of reflections, but which often presented themselves in my sense of being unable to cope with the situation if the class refused to listen to me. There is little point in repeating here the obvious, but inconsequential answers to such a fear. But the vital point is that I believe it was my increasing reliance upon trying to express how I felt on paper that was a major factor in enabling me to grow through this period. I quote from an extract:

> March 9th
> I think that my ambivalence to the role of authority in teaching is clarifying itself . . . . Last Tuesday when Chris (a pupil) said that I wouldn't make a teacher because of the lack of discipline in my lesson with 4Hj – I was nagged by what he had said. I had thought it was a very successful lesson, and yet it seemed I didn't have the courage of my convictions to deny Chris' remark . . . despite my rationalisations this anxiety continued.

> I then spent about three sides of paper concentrating upon trying to express some kind of survey of particular experiences in class and the staffroom, quoting comments and episodes. It is not a neutral record, but an expression of how I felt about particular experiences. Nevertheless it does not attempt to fit them all together into some kind of safe pattern which could escape the problems involved. I conclude by evaluating what I have done.

This whole process of reflection upon my experience is an interesting one, . . . symbolising my thoughts and anxieties in words is very helpful. I sometimes worry that this evades the experience itself by rationalising it, and this is always in tension. But I also think it makes some kind of sense of those anxieties which while inchoate threaten my calm and obsess my mind, denying other possibilities. In understanding comes a distancing and growing through these problems – fundamental changes. Not evading them – but hopefully locating them within a certain perspective – so that I may in beginning to 'know'/describe them think of ways of dealing with them and liberating the rest of my experience. (I suppose this is the major principle of psychoanalysis.) So that I am not helplessly at the mercy of my anxieties, seemingly surrounded by them, but able to face them as *an* aspect of my experience, which I may take positive action to change.

This seems very related to English teaching and the possibility of liberating kids by giving them a chance to understand their experience through language – most intensely perhaps 'poetic' language. The exorcising of one's emotional fears and sadness in poetry that I have often pursued.[22]

The relevance of this description to my argument will be readily discerned. Let us put it in some sort of schematic order. The student is suffering from an intense feeling of anxiety which is expressed in a number of overwhelming 'reflections'. Rational arguments do not touch the source of the emotion or restrain its power. The only activity which meets the anxiety is a consciously expressive one – the writing down of all that relates to the feeling. The expressive act brings about 'a distancing' and a 'growing through' the emotion by placing it 'within a certain perspective'. The excerpts in the journal are not art but the process, as the student perceives it, seems to parallel the artistic process, the integration of experience through 'poetic language'.

The second example I wish to look at concerns the composition of a ballad. As with the passage above, Edwin Muir's account of the genesis of a particular ballad begins with a negative and excessive emotion only to issue years later as an unconsciously formed poem. In his *An Autobiography*, Edwin Muir describes how at the age of seven he ran away from a certain Freddie Sinclair who threatened to fight him. He ran with an inordinate sense of fear and, as he felt he was being watched by people in the village, a sense of shame. According to Muir it took him thirty years to come to terms with the sense of dread and panic experienced on that afternoon. The account the poet gives is highly pertinent to our theme and it must be quoted at some length:

I got rid of that terror almost thirty years later in a poem describing Achilles chasing Hector round Troy, in which I pictured Hector returning after his death to run the deadly race over again. In the poem I imagined Hector as noticing with intense, dreamlike precision certain little things, not the huge simplified things which my conscious memory tells me I noticed in my own flight. The story is put in Hector's mouth:

The grasses puff a little dust
Where my footsteps fall,
I cast a shadow as I pass
The little wayside wall.

The strip of grass on either hand
Sparkles in the light,

I only see that little space
To the left and to the right.

And in that space our shadows run
His shadow there and mine
The little knolls, the tossing weeds,
The grasses frail and fine.

That is how the image came to me, quite spontaneously: I wrote the poem down, almost complete, at one sitting. But I have wondered since whether the intense concentration on little things, seen for a moment as the fugitive fled past them, may not be a deeper memory of that day preserved in a part of the mind which I cannot tap for ordinary purposes. In any case the poem cleared my conscience. I saw that my shame was a fantastically elongated shadow of a childish moment, imperfectly remembered; an untapped part of my mind supplied what my conscious recollection left out, and I could at last see the incident whole by seeing it as happening, on a great and tragic scale, to some one else. After I had written the poem the flight itself was changed, and with that my feelings towards it.[23]

In Muir's case the inner emotion crystallises in the rhythm of the ballad and the story of a mythical contest. 'My feeling', Muir went on to explain, 'about the Achilles and Hector poem is not of a suppression suddenly removed, but rather of something which has worked itself out'. The emotionally fraught incident is given objective form through mythic imagery and, as a result, understood in a new way, integrated into the psyche. 'The flight itself was changed' though the symbolic act 'and with that my feelings towards it'.

In the case of Edwin Muir the autonomous psychic process and the art-process are all but one. The poem is given to the conscious mind already complete; it is merely lifted like a ready-made figure out of the sea of the unconscious. In this sense it is not truly typical of the art-process which, as we shall see later, is more often a prolonged encounter between the expressive impulse and the artistic medium. In this encounter the medium in turn meets the impulse and contributes, like a lover, its own resistances, possibilities, inclinations. The creative tussle lies between the impulse and the medium; a tussle in which the medium has to submit to the creative impulse but in which in the struggle the impulse itself is modified, extended, even qualitatively changed. At high moments, there is a resolution and expressive form is realized. What was within the art-maker has been put out there in the world, a new born child, awaiting recognition and appreciation and criticism. Yet it is imperative to stress that the activity of making and the activity of responding to what is made do not take place in a vacuum. The art-maker lives in a culture, within a heritage; whether he regards himself as a traditionalist or an iconoclast he cannot escape the meanings which surround him. Even if he is reacting against, he is learning from his culture. He needs these meanings in order to make his meaning. His audience, too, live in the same culture, within a comparable net of shared assumptions, associations, expectations. It is through this common cultural background that the new work of art in the foreground of consciousness can develop in the artist and be recognized, at least to some degree, by the audience gathered to respond to it. We will return to this continuous activity of cultural mimesis later in the chapter.

It is time to examine more carefully the various stages of the art-making process, but let me first present our case so far in a series of propositions.

FIRST PROPOSITION
Art as a discipline of making is primarily devoted to the conversion of engaging impulse into expressive symbol; a symbol which embodied in a specific medium partly reflects and to varying degrees transforms the original impulse.

SECOND PROPOSITION
In making through expressive representation the art-maker matures through his experience, transforming impulse into vision and meaning.

THIRD PROPOSITION
That this process may, in part, be seen as an extending and deepening of biological activity in which emotion and instinct spontaneously manifest themselves as dream, image and phantasmagoria.

FOURTH PROPOSITION
The symbolic form (poem, novel, sculpture, dance, composition, painting, play, etc.) makes objective what was previously subjective, and as object it enters a public world where it can be experienced and evaluated by others.

FIFTH PROPOSITION
This process of making and evaluating does not happen in isolation but inside a social and cultural milieux where certain practices and certain traditions have been long established.

With these five propositions boldly before us, I will now describe the five phases of the art-making process.

IV

In his autobiography *Memories, Dreams, Reflections* Carl Jung briefly states why, as a pupil, he was unable to respond to his art classes:

> I was exempted from drawing classes on grounds of utter incapacity. This in a way was welcome to me, since it gave me more free time; but on the other hand it was a fresh defeat, since I had some facility in drawing, although I did not realise that it depended essentially on the way I was feeling. I could draw only what stirred my imagination. But I was forced to copy prints of Greek gods with sightless eyes, and when that wouldn't go properly the teacher obviously thought I needed something more naturalistic and set before me the picture of a goat's head. This assignment I failed completely, and that was the end of my drawing classes.[24]

Jung's case is representative of so many individuals who later when the springs of the art-making process were unexpectedly released found, to their great satisfaction, that they actually had an ability to express their feelings in the very medium from which they had once been formally excluded or judged as wanting by their teachers. It is deeply ironical that Jung who as a child sat for hours in front of the paintings at the Klein-Huningen parsonage, 'gazing at all this beauty' and who was later to restore the place of the gods to the human imagination could not respond to the prints of the Greek gods in his drawing classes. Yet, as he indicates, the reason was simple enough; no feeling was released and without feeling there could be no creative act, only a sterile imitation. Like so many teachers of the expressive disciplines, Jung's teacher had found a way of developing certain mechanical skills which by-passed the expressive task altogether.

Impulse is the pulse of art-making, rooted in the body and moving outwards. To exclude impulse is to exclude the very source of art-making. For it is impulse which bears the energy necessary for the creation of new symbols. As we have suggested, within impulse there is a desire for reflection, a desire for an image which will hold, comprehend and complete. This desire is buried in the body, bound into our instincts, an innate propensity. Art is the life of the body, projected, developed and taken into consciousness.

The art-making process, thus, begins with an impulse which taken into a particular medium struggles to develop itself, to give shape to itself, to recognise its latent meanings. It is not, as has often been claimed, a question of emotional discharge or of displacement of emotion or of some therapeutic release. Such phrases presuppose an essentially negative view of emotion. It is rather a question of following through an impulse in order to comprehend its meaning. It is to do with passionate reflection. What we are describing is a process which has a fair chance of culminating in knowledge, in the cognition of human nature and an evaluation of that nature. Art is, thus, an epistemological activity, one of the most subtle agents we have for the realisation of the perennial injunction: 'Know thyself and be thyself'. In the English tradition, John Stuart Mill fleetingly recognised the philosophical importance of art when in a letter to Carlyle he wrote:

> for it is the artist alone in whose hands Truth becomes impressive and a living principle of action

> . . . the poet or artist is coversant chiefly with such (intuitive) truths and that his office in respect to truth is to declare them and to make them impressive . . . . By him alone is real knowledge of such truths conveyed.[25]

And it was, later, Collingwood who in the closing paragraph of *The Principles of Art* gave such a magnificent defence of the arts in their power to keep consciousness true:

> The artist must prophesy not in the sense that he fortells things to come, but in the sense that he tells his audience, at risk of their displeasure, the secrets of their own hearts. His business as an artist is to speak out, to make a clean breast. But what he has to utter is not, as the individualistic theory of art would have us think, his own secrets. As spokesman of his community, the secrets he must utter are theirs. The reason why they need him is that no community altogether knows its own heart; and by failing in this knowledge a community deceives itself on the one subject concerning which ignorance means death. For the evils which come from that ignorance the poet as prophet suggests no remedy, because he has already given one.

> The remedy is the poem itself. Art is the community's medicine for the worst disease of mind, the corruption of consciousness.[26]

At the same time as we recognise this philosophical dimension to the arts we must not forget that art-making is a wholly natural activity, an astonishing outgrowth of instinct. Its blossom may open out in consciousness but its roots are down deep in effective impulse, in muscular and nervous rhythms, the beat of the heart, the intake and release of breath, patterns of perception, unconscious coordination of the limbs, the obscure, fluctuating, dimly sensed movements of the organism, in the preconceptual play of the psyche.

The release of impulse, then, forms the first phase of the creative process. There is a stirring of the psyche which through expression desires clarification and integration. The second phase of the movement can be discerned when the impulse grapples with a particular medium for its full representation and in the encounter develops further its own nature. As we know, this can be a prolonged activity with its outcome uncertain. Only occasionally does the material in the hands of the maker shape itself immediately to the pattern of the informing impulse. It is worth noticing here that the word medium to denote expressive form or materials remains somewhat deceptive as the word too easily suggests (as in its spiritualist use) an open space through which a force passes, a neutral passage for the vehicles of creative intention. But in the expressive disciplines the medium is not simply neutral, open or passive. The medium has its own inner propensities, its own laws, its own history. It allows and forbids. It invites and resists. It may or may not yield the authentic representation we seek. The impulse can be lost in the material, can be betrayed by the material or, at high moments, taken to an unexpected consummation. Certainly, the second phase of the art-making process is the most problematic of all.

Let us consider a little more carefully the relationship between impulse and medium, taking language as our example. The words the writer uses to convey his experience are not his own; they have been inherited; they belong to the culture and he relies on them to make his personal meanings communal. The words carry distinct qualities, deposits built up over the centuries, condensations of collective responses to experiences, wise responses, foolish responses, responses more-or-less adequate, responses wholly inadequate but nevertheless recorded and passed on. *The language is not a neutral medium.* It can ensnare the writer. How often, for example, do we write about a particular feeling only to admit 'But that isn't it at all. That is another state of mind, not mine'? The habits of the established language take over the impulse and confer upon it an alien sense. And yet how tempting it can be to accept the given formulation because, while it may feel wrong, *it sounds right*. It sounds so acceptable because it has been safely established as a language pattern. Because it conveys what has been commonly established, it takes an extraordinary amount of stubborness to resist the false meaning that has appeared to crystallise within an emerging impulse. The spontaneous work of art is frequently no more than the gushing forth of unconsciously assimilated clichés and platitudes. In such cases the medium is, paradoxically, in tyrannical control and the original impulse submerged, almost from birth, in the miasma of received opinions. Nevertheless it is also true that, at other times, the words can take the writer deeper than he anticipated so that the impulse is given a depth and resonance which is, at once, infallibly right and yet seems to possess so much more than the initial upsurge of feeling promised. Here, in contrast, the language richly contributes to the expression of the original impulse giving it a quality and meaning it could not have had prior to expression. Just as there is no neutral impulse, so there is no neutral medium; the encounter between the two demands the most refined discrimination. Only by loving and hating and coming to know his medium can the art-maker hope to discover the full import of his impulses and thus make patent the latent self, the self which longs to be.

The way artists describe this phase of art-making is revealing. We read accounts which dramatise the aggressive nature of the act; thus we hear of the artist's *struggle*, his *wrestling* with the materials, his *attacking* the canvas, of his *dominating* or *subduing, manipulating* or *capturing* his subject-matter; of his *forging* a language; but we also hear of artists who gently *allow*, who *coax*, who *submit to*, who quietly *attend to*, let *unfold*, become *receptive channels for*. In the creative act both masculine and feminine dispositions are called for. Sometimes, the art-maker has to passively listen to the material or receive the impulse. At other times, he must actively convert the invisible throb of impulse into the visible language of art. The difficulties have been well caught by T. S. Eliot:

> Words strain
> Crack and sometimes break, under the burden,
> Under the tension, slip, slide and perish
> Decay with imprecision, will not stay in place
> Will not stay still.[27]

In this second phase of art-making the individual is striving to embody his experience, to make it not only personal but also representative. He moves from first approximations, from notes and highly-charged fragments, towards that which is progressively more shaped, more completely expressive. As the work develops, so his critical judgement comes more fully into play. He begins to discard, to select, to consider, to evaluate. Dryden described the process succinctly when he referred to one of his plays:

> Long before it was a play, when it only was a confused mess of thoughts, trembling over one another in the dark; when the fancy was yet in its first work, moving the sleeping images of things towards the light, these to be distinguished, and then either chosen or rejected by the judgement.[28]

Towards the end of this second phase of art-making, the critical judgement, which has to be in abeyance or severely inhibited in the first stages of creative work, slowly comes into its own. This coincides with a subtle but distinct shift in attention from a preoccupation with immediate approximate expression to a preoccupation with final representative form. As the work moves towards completion the art-maker will frequently consult with an imagined audience, constantly seeking its advice: 'How does this bit look?' 'Should it be this way round?' 'Is the reference too obscure?' 'Does it go on too long?' 'Is it finished?' It is as if a continuous inner dialogue is taking place between the artist and critic, between the creative subject and the sympathetic onlooker. And through this often harrowing interrogation, the work, if all goes well, attains its definitive shape. In some circumstances, of course, the critical voice is not only inside the art-maker, it is also out there, in the close friend, a fellow artist, a guiding tutor. But the common concern for an outside viewpoint suggests a truth about art-making which needs stressing: it is not only a personal activity it is also impersonal and has a communicative and communal intention. Art is a public category. What is made by the art-maker, and particularly that which is made well, requires the recognition of a community. On the one side, the art-maker, if his work is to mature, needs an audience; he needs its regard, its appreciation and its criticism. He needs to know whether he has achieved representative form, whether he has succeeded in capturing the essential truth of the human impulse. On the other side, the community for its health and wholeness, needs to attend to the truths which the art-maker, defiantly or tentatively, holds up for its reflection.

Thus, the art-making process does not end when the paints are returned to their boxes, the pen put down, the plaster and clay droppings swept into the corner; these actions only mark the ending of one crucial sequence. The next sequence, of equal importance, takes the artefact into the world in search of that audience the art-maker has already imagined and addressed in the heat of the creative act. In fact, an analysis of the entire process of art-making discloses a characteristic movement from subjective to objective, from self to other, from private to public, from self-expression to representative embodiment. Here we can begin to see how the Progressive's insistence on 'self-expression', the Cambridge School's emphasis on 'discrimination' and the Socio-Linguist's concern for 'audience' represent partial truths which can be given their full meaning only when they are brought into relationship with the whole complex pattern of art-making. Dislocated from this broad context, however, they can become dangerously misleading. 'Self-expression' may be valuable in the initial stages of art-making but it does not convey the ultimate goal of the activity for it excludes both the principles of representative embodiment and of a trans-personal communication. Art has much to do with 'self' and with 'expression', but it also has much to do with discipline, form, structure, objectivity, community and cultural inheritance. 'Discrimination' likewise is an essential element but only in its fitting place. Too much discrimination, too soon, and the source of authentic art dries up. The art-maker, in Dryden's words, must first freely invite 'the confused mass of thoughts, trembling over one another in the dark' into consciousness before he can begin to coherently select and shape. First indiscriminate expression ('self-expression'); then discriminate making ('representative embodiment'). It is similar with the need for an 'audience'. Art may be consummated in its electric transmission to an audience, but before this can happen the art-maker needs a protected space, an enclave, without ideological pressure, in which he can give mankind's confused mass of struggling impulses a habitation and a name:

> That girls at puberty may find
> The first Adam in their thoughts,
> Shut the door of the Pope's chapel

Keep those children out
There on that scaffolding reclines
Michael Angelo
With no more sound than the mice make
His hand moves to and fro
Like a long-legged fly upon the stream
His mind moves upon silence.[29]

The art-maker serves an audience but to serve it well he must serve, first, a deeper impulse in his own nature. As Collingwood rightly declared he is not an entertainer, not a magician, not a propagandist. And the art-maker must be constantly on his guard against an audience that might seduce him into any one of these three pseudo-roles. Yet, as Yeats insists, the artist labours for the illumination of others, for the enlargement of consciousness. As we have seen, there is a reciprocal relationship of need between the art-maker and his audience.

The fourth phase of the art-making process, then, takes what has been made (and judged as sufficiently representative by the maker) into the community. The work calls for presentation, for performance. The painting or sculpture needs exhibiting, the poetry needs disseminating, the music needs playing. Such presentations can demand creative energy of the highest order. Indeed, in the case, say, of musical performance, the performers become co-authors of the work. The performer has to re-create the artefact, enter it with his own personality, relive it and embody it for a living audience. It is a healthy sign that we have recently begun talking about 'the performing arts' for such a description italicizes the public face of art and rightly suggests that the performer is an artist in his own right. His activity too is central to our conception of the expressive disciplines. It is his function to bring the truth of the emotion as determined by the art home to the society. Through presentations (exhibitions, publications) and through performances (concerts, recitals, dance, theatre, public readings) the art-work is taken out into the world until, at best, it enters the imagination of the human race.

The response of the audience and, particularly, of the immediate audience is also an essential part of the art-making process. If the performer is co-author of a work so, to some extent, is the audience. An audience, as we all know from first-hand experience, can 'bring out' or 'freeze' a performance. A collaborative audience is all but a necessary condition for good art. The audience is not just a hollow receptacle or the terminal station on the long route of art-making, although in an age of mass-culture, this so easily happens. A mass audience cannot contribute to any process, nor can the instant electronic communication to millions of distracted individuals nurture the arts. When the art-maker addressed the audience of his imagination, it was a united audience, an engaged audience, an identifiable audience possessing passion, intelligence and disarming honesty. It must be so because he needs to learn from it. So it should be with the audience 'out there' – it needs to be intimate, collaborative and forthright. Without such an audience art can quickly deteriorate into consumer fodder (as with most books, most music, most film, most theatre, most art) or solitary masturbation. Without such an audience art becomes what we largely have, anartism. The final stage of the art-making process lies with the audience, in their response to and evaluation of the art that has been produced. Do the forms embody the secrets of their own hearts? Does the art delight, disturb, reveal the enduring lineaments of the psyche? Does it tell the human truth, however darkly strange and demanding? Or is it sham? Ego writ large? Mere cosmopolitan flash? Or is it caught in the very platitudes from which individuals struggle to free themselves, looking at art for the wider meaning? Without a discriminating audience, the integrity demanded by the earlier art-making phases is liable to falter and fail.

V

Our account of art-making discloses five essential phases which can be schematically delineated in spiral motion as follows:

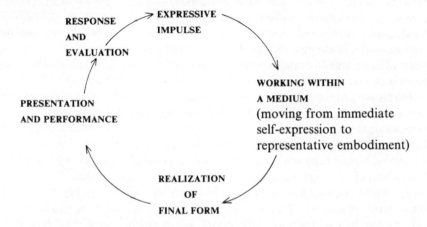

The phases placed in such a schematic spiral relationship represent an idealized sequence. It has not been my intention to plot the separate itineraries of each art-form (the differences emerging from the marked differences between the media) but rather to point to the common nature of the journey. Later I want to register certain qualifications about the application of such a schema to the teaching of the arts, but at this point I want to take the argument a stage further by placing the foreground of the creative process against the general background of cultural mimesis through which the art-maker absorbs, uses and learns from all that exists in the culture, and through a continuous assimilation, masters and transforms. We need, in other words, to see the five phases of art-making as working within an endless dialectic between inherited form and emergent process.

The artist is not an autist. He creates out of his impulses but he can only create through his culture. Let me give one example. For decades Van Gogh has been the stereotype for the manic genius, the solitary creator of an individual vision. Yet this stereotype is hopelessly out of relationship with the actual truth of Van

Gogh's life. This is not the place to make the argument in detail but any cursory acquaintance with the letter of Van Gogh reveals a man immersed in culture. Not only does he warmly discuss the literary work of Tolstoy, Dickens, Zola, Carlyle, Maupassant, Whitman, George Eliot, Shakespeare and Goethe, he also shows the keenest appreciation of innumerable painters: of, for example, Monticelli, Daumier, Gericault, Delacroix, Millet, Rembrandt, Rousseau, Courbet and Giotto. He encounters certain Japanese prints and his work immediately absorbs the influence. Writing to Theo in 1888 about the painting of his bedroom he claims 'it is coloured in free flat tones like Japanese prints'. He sees Gauguin's work and, again, it has an immediate effect on the form of his own work. The original painter sees himself in traditional terms. From Saint-Rémy, a year before his death, he writes to his brother (who represented the only community he ever had) 'When I realize the worth and originality and the superiority of Delacroix and Millet, for instance, then I am bold to say – yes, I am something, I can do something. *But I must have a foundation in those artists*, and then produce the little "which I am capable of in the same direction".' (My italics). The art grows out of the culture as well as out of the deep impulses of self: the two are inextricably intertwined. Identity without culture is a definition of autism. Culture without identity defines the closed totalitarian state. Furthermore, in Van Gogh we find an example of a man who is driven to suicidal despair because he cannot find a living community for the culture he has made.

The creative process takes place inside a culture where the forms of the past are constantly recreated and recast. As we claimed earlier, the seed of impulse must be sown into the rich humus of culture or, at least, the richest we can manage. It was the fallacy of the Progressive School to posit a 'pure' individual who was 'naturally' creative and who, as it were, created works of art merely by breathing. The notion of 'self-expression' as an absolute aim derives from an indulgent and insupportable view of human nature. To create we have invariably, to imitate. Poesis requires mimesis. We need to know what others have done and how they have done it. In teaching the arts, therefore, we need to grapple with the historical dimension of culture-making but always in terms of living impulse and existential need. In this way the culture grows into the child, the child into the culture; the present roots itself into the past, the past flows, renewed, into the present. In the next chapter I will describe the implications of mimesis for the teaching of English as a literary-expressive discipline. Here I raise it to suggest the encompassing framework within which and through which individual creativity operates and develops. The notion of mimesis raises a further problem about art-making for we live in a society where the dominant forms of culture are corrupt, designed not to reveal but to conceal, not to illuminate but to exploit. Such a condition makes the teaching of all the arts problematic. Nevertheless the principle of mimesis holds. We have no choice but to engage with contemporary forms in an attempt to turn them into fresh material for revelation and embodied insight. We must throw the junk of the consumer society into the furnace of the imagination in order to transmute, in order to create forms which correspond more closely to the authentic impulses of our children and adolescents. The existing metaphors of our society demand, even more than the traditions we receive from the past, the habits of creative mimesis. The danger is that we become corrupted by the very symbolism we seek to transform. Sinking so low, we cut our chances of flying high. Nevertheless if we are to transcend consumer-culture, we must first penetrate it. To leave it out of account in our teaching, is to leave its power untouched and unchecked.

The creative act does not take place in a vacuum. The symbol is the *sine qua non* of all the expressive disciplines and in the symbol the self and the community struggle to meet.

I want now to consider the value of the concepts I have developed in this chapter for the teaching of the expressive disciplines. It is hoped they go some way towards providing a common language across the arts and, through the language, a shared understanding. I think they enable us to see where our teaching in the arts often goes wrong. Used with great sensitivity they also provide tools for an analysis of classroom practice. I want first to raise some general reflections about the arts in schools and then, with the aid of the art-making schema, make a more specific analysis of how art-teachers perceive their own teaching practice.

Jung's art-teacher was no exception. Innumerable teachers then and now demand creative work without ever releasing an expressive need, a generative impulse in their pupils. In English, for example, a title can be simply announced or scribbled on the board and the class expected, within a certain allocated time, to provide an animated story or poetic narrative. There is often no attempt to free an impulse, sufficiently urgent to break through the enclosing walls of platitudes and dreary commonplaces. In most of the expressive disciplines, teachers fail to stimulate in their students a prolonged experimental encounter with the medium, do not encourage a professional sense of work in process; do not convey the sense that revision may well constitute the messy path to vision. There is also often a grudging attitude to wastage, a cramped, narrow, restrictive view as regards materials. The following remarks by an art-teacher to his students reveal the generous explorative spirit of good arts teaching (though in some teaching contexts the hectoring almost bullying tone might be dangerously amiss):

> Take a look at her. Sitting there like a great, fat, rolling Buddha! Bloody marvellous, she is. And look what you've made her. Call that drawing? Puny, little scratches. Scrap it. Get yourself a decent sheet of paper. Pin it on the wall . . . and a pot of black ink and brush. Then go at it. Get into her. Make her alive. Stop caring. All right, you make a mess of it. Take another sheet. Have another go. But for Christ's sake, give it all you've got . . . .[30]

Many teachers just fail to take their students through any formative experience.

As Witkin pointed out in *The Intelligence of Feeling*, one of the reasons for this failure is that teachers having started a creative activity are reluctant to intervene; they stand nervously on the side lines isolated from the activity, inwardly praying that they will not be called into the ring. But it is important that the teacher is able to enter the creative act, to know what stage the pupil may have reached and therefore what kind of problems he is likely to be engaging with. At times, the pupil may require technical help and then it is essential that the teacher can introduce the required technique in such a way that it bears upon the informing impulse. As an English teacher I have looked through innumerable exercise books full of stories which each time have merely received some ejaculatory remark: 'Good', 'Poor', 'An improvement', 'Excellent'; remarks given without any indication as to what elements make it good (and how they could be developed further) or what elements make it weak (and how they could be re-handled). It must lead the pupil to conclude that, after all, creative work is only a fancy label for another exercise in which neatness, number of words and a certain plausability count.

It is also the case that many teachers in the arts fail to envisage the class, the school and the neighbourhood as the obvious community for the art-work. Too often the original poem lies like a crushed butterfly caught between the pages of some drab exercise book, the sensitive sketch lies lost beneath a dusty pile of sugar-paper, the unusual play goes unrecorded and unperformed. How many English departments, even when they have ready access to cheap photo-litho printing machines, bring out with some degree of regularity novels, essays, poems, reviews selected from their pupils' work? How many art departments arrange exhibitions in local cafes, post offices, libraries and other public or private institutions? How many even ensure that the best art and sculpture forms an inescapable part of the school environment? How many music departments compose music, let alone perform it at school assembly or in local arts festivals? And yet, as we have seen, the art-maker requires an encompassing context for the development of his work.

The schema I have put forward in this chapter may be valuable in identifying areas which are being neglected in the teaching of the expressive disciplines. Through a rapid series of observations and questions I have tried to indicate where some of the weaknesses lie. Ultimately, the problem is a pedagogic one – for sensitive teaching of the arts should imaginatively meet the various demands of each phase. Yet it is clear from discussions and interviews that many teachers have a very truncated understanding of the art-process and so inevitably do harm when teaching, substituting mechanical imitation for emotional representation, craft for art, clever know-how for authenticity of response, competitive competitions for communal exhibitions. Yet a significant minority of teachers do have an excellent grasp of the intrinsic value of aesthetic activity and teach with acumen and delight, as we shall now see.

VI

In this section I propose to quote a number of comments art teachers in a middle school recently made about their work and then to comment on them in the light of the concepts developed in this chapter. The comments have been taken from an MA dissertation (for the University of Sussex) examining the teaching of art in one middle school in the south of England. The teachers, of course, represent only themselves. They may or may not be representative of teachers working nationally at this level. My main purpose is to bring the art-making schema into critical and interpretive relationship with what art teachers, at least in this highly specific context, claimed to be doing. I will quote the particular teacher at some length and then briefly offer a diagnosis in terms of the concepts introduced in this chapter.

PASSAGE AND DIAGNOSIS

TEACHER'S COMMENTARY A

One of the real problems with art is thinking of new things for the children to do. On this occasion I was in the staff-room talking to one of the supply teachers who always has lots of ideas for art. She suggested 'butterflies' because they were usually fairly successful. I drew the shape of the body for them on the blackboard and told them that I wanted a really colourful picture. I do like art work to be bold and colourful. I also encourage them to give their work a black outline because otherwise it just doesn't show up when it's on the wall.

This is an artistic class who mostly produce work that is good enough to go on the wall. They have produced a lot of lovely work that they have taken home, I wish you could have seen it. There is not much up at the moment but those 'butterflies' are a good example of the type of thing we do. They did those for a competition. I run quite a lot of competitions because the children enjoy them and think that they are fun. The winners get prizes, just team points you know for their team, but they like that. I always find it so difficult to pick the winners so I usually ask someone else to come and judge them – for example a colleague or one of the ancillary staff.

DIAGNOSIS

In terms of the art-making schema, the teacher does not engender an impulse (the theme is simply given: butterflies) nor does she encourage any experimental grappling with the medium. There is no exploration of the material: the colours are largely dictated as is the actual shape. ('I . . . told them that I wanted a really colourful picture. I do like art work to be bold and colourful'.) The teacher knows what she wants the children to make; it is more like a mass manufacturing than a personal creating. No impulse (first phase) is released; there is no exploratory self-expression within the medium (opening of the second phase) and no personal struggle towards representative form (development of the second phase culminating in the realisation of final form).

However, the last two phases of our schema are strongly in evidence. The bounding black line is suggested because of its presentational qualities, 'otherwise it just doesn't show up when it's on the wall'. The problem here lies with *what* is being presented and *how* it is being evaluated. In the absence of the first three phases, the last two become an appalling parody of what they should be about. Spurious art is receiving a collective validation. The colleague or ancillary staff member is brought in not to judge the aesthetic embodiment of personal impulse but rather to select from a set of standarized images. The researcher described 'the winners' as possessing 'a certain amount of technical proficiency' and 'a fairly symmetrical if rather stylised form'.

It is also well worth noting that the emotional excitement which should run within the expressive activity is brought in *from outside*; the sense of 'fun' is imported by the externalities of competition, house-points and prizes. Thus, we witness the very reverse of what has been delineated in this chapter. Instead of emergent tentative emotion being explored through an expressive medium and refined into representative form, we find an alien collective emotion being brought to bear upon the art-making process to sponsor visual clichés. Mind-forged manacles are being fastened upon the children's imaginations with an accompanying sense of 'fun' for the awaiting prizes and team points. In the art lesson, art comes to an end.

PASSAGE AND DIAGNOSIS

TEACHER'S COMMENTARY B

Actually I don't do all that much art because, well, with more than thirty children in a room this size it is really difficult to organise. There is only one small sink and you usually find that everyone wants to use it at once, so we hardly ever do any painting for instance. We are meant to have one art lesson a week but I often miss it and use the time to illustrate topic work instead. I do think that creativity and self-expression are important but the children really need to learn skills as well, so when I do have art I usually concentrate on that side of it.

DIAGNOSIS

A perplexing proposition: I regard self-expression as of such importance that I arrange the day so that it never takes place.

Notice the immediate linking of 'creativity' and 'self-expression', this deceptive correlation coming through from the Progressive Movement as defined in the first chapter. In our analysis 'self-expression' is only one facet of the creative act.

Notice also the emphasis on skills dislocated from informing impulses. In our analysis skills are essential but are seen to serve a deeper primary activity of questing, of finding meaning. Skills do not exist 'as well' as expression, they exist within the expressive act in order that expression may become embodied, inwardly grasped and outwardly communicated.

PASSAGE AND DIAGNOSIS

TEACHER'S COMMENTARY C

This class is less artistically creative than the one I had last year, in fact they are not very keen on Art at all. I use the television programme that we watch, as a starting point for some of their art, but most of it is related to class topic work in History, Maths and Nature. I think really that the art they have done for nature has been the best this term. I find that the more intelligent children are more critical of their art work and become very frustrated if they can't get their work to look realistic. They need to use pictures more in order to learn to observe more accurately. I encourage them to copy from pictures because I think that they need to develop observation skills.

DIAGNOSIS

The key assumption here is that art is imitation, the 'realistic' reproduction of three dimensional objects on two dimensional surfaces. Such a view has a long tradition in our civilisation. It is there, for example, in Leonardo de Vinci who wrote 'without perspective nothing can be done well in any kind of painting'. It is given its strongest philosophical formulation in Plato's *Republic*, where the artist is envisaged as making a copy of that which already exists. Such a view still has a strong hold on the popular consciousness. It is still widely felt that art has 'to construct an illusion of space through which objects' can 'be seen in perspectival coherence'. In the classroom it can result in an obsession with realism which quickly deteriorates, as in the practice of the school in question, into lifeless copying and even worse, tracing.

The aim of this chapter has been partly to assert a fundamentally different concept of art as the symbolic expression and clarification of inward impulse. When I have used the concept 'representative form' I have not meant to imply *representational accuracy* (which may or may not be important depending upon the painter's needs) but to denote *the incarnation of the creative impulse in the chosen medium*. T. S. Eliot referred to this as 'the objective correlative'. With such a broad conception of art-making we are able to see why the concern in the above account for 'observation skills' and 'realistic' art is misplaced. It is narrowing art to a technique for securing representational images rather than a living process through which experience is given shape and coherence. At some point a desire for representative form may well require perspective; then the teacher has to bring representational technique to bear upon the student's impulse. But art is not a matter of knowing how to achieve a mathematical recession of figures across a flat surface.

In terms of our art-making schema the teacher would seem not to allow, in any significant manner, for any of the five phases. One is left with the strong suspicion that art is not being developed as an expressive discipline but being used mechanically as an illustrative tool for other disciplines. A widespread habit in our primary and middle schools.

PASSAGE AND DIAGNOSIS

TEACHER'S COMMENTARY D

I do take art with my class once a week, but no, I don't consider that it is as important as other subjects in the curriculum. We (both second year classes) watch a weekly television programme and that has some guidelines for follow up work on art. We also have a radio programme about nature and we use that for art quite often as well. Last week it was about elephants and so, as you can see, they did some pictures about that. Some children drew their elephant from imagination and memory, others copied from pictures (photographs) that were in the pamphlets that go with the broadcasts. If I have a child with a flair for art I let them do their own thing, but usually the children need a lot of guidance and instruction on techniques.

DIAGNOSIS

Here again we find:

(a) reliance on outer machinery to start the art-lesson

(b) widespread practice of passive copying

(c) no appreciation of the importance of art in education

(d) few of the phases described in this chapter allowed for and none developed

(e) no interception into the creative process. Children with flair are 'allowed to do their own thing'. In this case, no doubt, a fortunate omission. But how can such pupils develop?

PASSAGE AND DIAGNOSIS

TEACHER'S COMMENTARY E

I do take them for some art lessons, mainly because as a subject I enjoy it so much myself. They go to Mrs Peters to work with clay. I do use art in an integrated way, too, relating it to other subjects, but it is important in its own right as well. I know that art is often thought of as the traditional 'playtime' activity but I think that self-expression is very important. Art is a totally creative thing. Skills are important of course, and necessary. Knowing how to mould clay, bang a nail, mix paint are essential preliminaries to self-expression, but they are only preliminaries. I think that art helps in a way to teach self-reliance and to give the child self-confidence, well, that is what I work towards. I try to make them think about their own response in art. When they come to me and say 'Is it right?' I say to them 'Is that what you wanted to do?' I also encourage them to justify their own opinions about art. If one of them criticises or praises another child's work or even comments on their own art I always ask them to tell me why they like or dislike it. My specialism is science and I am very aware of the difference between the way I am teaching the children to think in art compared with science. It is something that I try to make the children aware of too. I tell them that recording in art is very different from science – it is to do with expression. I also try to give the children quite a wide experience with different media. There is some paper sculpture over there and these strange faces and people that they have painted arose out of some work that was totally imaginative in origin, based on the idea of a 'super hero'. They do quite a lot of still life work too. Another aspect of art that I try to introduce them to is the work of famous artists. I used to borrow some slides from the College of Art, but they stopped lending them eventually. Many of these children have no artistic background at home and no idea about different painters and styles, and I think that they should know a little about their culture. I don't show them pictures very often but I really just want to say to them – 'Look, this is what people do'.

DIAGNOSIS

Although we find in the above a reference to 'self-expression', the overall context indicates a more complex understanding of art. There is a fine recognition of the proper place of skill and a true appreciation of the disciplined expressive nature of art-making (seen to constitute a different kind of *thinking* from science). Although there is no specific description of how she begins her art lessons we can safely surmise that she works outwards from the desire to express. It is clear that the second phase is carefully attended to; the children are given 'a wide experience with different media' and urged to judge their work in terms of their own creative intentions, not, as in previous examples, in terms of preconceived demands.

There is also an appreciation of cultural understanding of the heritage. The children are asked to respond to paintings in the culture in a direct and unpretentious manner ('I really just want to say to them – 'Look this is what people do'.) Earlier in the chapter it was argued that 'The art-maker lives within a culture, within a heritage . . . . He needs those meanings in order to make his meanings'. In an unobtrusive manner the teacher is forging an immediate connection between the art in the classroom and the art that is in the tradition. She is providing the necessary conditions for creative mimesis. It is interesting to observe also the importance the teacher places on art as a means of self-reliance and self-confidence. This is not elaborated upon but could well be understood in the terms, presented earlier, of art being primarily concerned with the integration of impulse, and the differentiation of feeling in the evolving consciousness of the child.

Only one phase in the creative process would seem to be neglected; the presentation of what has been made in the art lesson to a community broader than the class.

PASSAGE AND DIAGNOSIS

TEACHER'S COMMENTARY F

I think that art is equally as important as other subjects and to neglect the creative and expressive side of education, to which art makes a unique contribution, is really to ignore one half of the child's educational needs. Art is about intuitive feeling, and helping the child to express his feelings creatively. I do think they need to have some skills and guidelines of course, but this should be provided in a framework without stifling them, so that they are still free to express themselves. In working with clay for example, some basic knowledge is essential, but I would call these 'Threshold skills' and I keep them to a minimum. These clay heads are nearly finished now, it has been going on for several weeks. I used one of the boys as a model to begin with and the children all sketched him. I think it is important that the children explore a stimulus thoroughly, experimenting with several types of media, before committing themselves to the final form. Sketching the model took most of the first lesson and they have also done a painting of the same subject. Sometimes I include printing as well but this time they followed the painting session with work in clay. But the subject is not so important as the child's interpretation of it. I am trying to help the child to focus his own feelings and personal reactions to the subject. It is important to start with the child and not with the subject.

DIAGNOSIS

Most of the key elements of art-making would seem to be in a vivid and fitting relationship. Skills are seen as serving and opening out expressive impulses. Experimentation with the medium is seen as the necessary preliminary to the realisation of 'final form'. And the importance of art-making in the education of feeling is clearly comprehended. Even the figure-work is seen to begin in the subject's response to the sitter, not to the task of photographic representation. Here is a teacher who has an understanding of Jung's insight that art depends on the rhythm of feeling and the stirring of imagination. We will have cause later to reflect on the practice of encouraging initial exploration in a variety of media before settling to one material. (For doesn't this express a principle which could be taken much further across all the expressive disciplines?)

In brief, although in the passage there is no mention of the concluding phases of art-making, we sense a teacher who has an admirable grasp of the intrinsic value of art as an expressive discipline.

VII

Our analysis indicates – no more than that – the kind of interpretive analysis made possible by the art-making schema. The dynamism of concepts reside in their power to open up actuality; they urge us to envisage an articulate sequence rather than a random series of instants, allow us to conceive a living totality rather than a disconnected mass of fragments. Yet concepts are not without their dangers; they can provide a rational ordering which, while plausible misses the essential point. The very purity of abstractions can seduce the reader into a false acceptance of a theory, which because of an internal consistency, seems intellectually binding. It is, therefore, important that the reader turn upon the schema and ruthlessly question it. What are its weaknesses? What does it leave out? What needs further amplification? What needs to be discarded? What are the alternatives? For myself I am passionately engaged in the argument. It has not been an academic exercise but a desire to understand a remarkable phenomena and to meet a great educational need which has driven me on. I am, therefore, not the best person to turn a sceptical energy upon the construction. I have been very conscious of trying to hold opposed but complementary forces together, that of the individual and that of the community, that of process and that of production, that of originating impulse and that of surrounding and received culture. I contend that our life is lived in the centre of these tensions and that any adequate theory of aesthetics must include both sides, must keep the painful, renewing dialectic in motion. Again and again, art-discourse and educational discourse slackens the tension by choosing one side at the expense of the other. The society is made dominant or the individual; the product is made dominant or the process. The history of drama teaching, like the history of dance, is split into factions which affirm a commitment to either expression or technique, process or production. It would be wrong not to observe the integrity which underlies many of these time-worn divisions, but it would also be foolish not to observe that, invariably, the factions *understood together* make up the essential meaning of the discipline. For art is both to do with the individual and with the society; with expression, representation, and communication. It is only by struggling for the synthesis of all the key elements that we can arrive at a more comprehensive understanding and, thereby, a fitting pedagogy.

I am not the best person to shake my own argument. Nevertheless I am anxious that the schema is not crudely imposed upon the living rhythms of experience. I want, therefore, to register a number of further reflections and qualifications. If it adds to the complexity, so much the better!

Firstly, as a schema it cannot possibly describe the unique process by which any individual creation is made or begin to suggest the delight, fear and trembling which attends its making. All it purports to do is to define conceptually the characteristic spiral pattern of art-making.

Secondly, although I have referred to impulse as the origin of the creative act it is nevertheless clearly the case that art-making can be initiated by simply playing with the medium (feeling the clay, making sounds, listing arbitrary words, limbering up with the body). In such instances the medium itself generates an expressive impulse which then turns back onto the medium with a sudden directed energy. Here, then, we find a new variation: medium —→ impulse —→ grappling with the medium —→ approximate form —→ realization of final form etc. Such a variation, however, in no way denies the generative importance of impulse.

Thirdly, the impulse and the symbol often seem to emerge simultaneously. Thus we do not always experience a discreet impulse followed by a symbolic form. The symbolic form often seems to reside within the impulse. The thought and the word, the feeling and the image are experienced together. Although this is true, nevertheless, the distinction can be conceptually discerned. We can, for example, all recognize when words are being used to fill a vacuum and when they are serving the energy of a creative impulse. Such impulses, rooted in the affective, give birth to art; that such impulses may be immediately experienced as sound, shape, imagery confirms my earlier notion that art is a biological activity and in no way negates the later *conceptual* delineation of art-making.

Fourthly, the emphasis placed on performance and evaluation must not be allowed to distort the first vulnerable exploratory stages of art-making. The intention is not to promote an artificial simulation of emotion for the pleasure of an amused audience but rather to create genuine art-making within a living community. It might well be that for a number of terms a particular class might concentrate entirely on the first phases of art-making; might, at times, concentrate only on the generation of approximate forms, of images in process. In certain cases, the teacher alone may have to represent the attentive audience and the quality of the creative work may depend entirely upon this protected, unconditionally trusted, single relationship. When it comes to performance to a larger community, it is of the utmost importance that this too is seen as a living process, demanding perhaps different imaginative qualities than the initial creation and often calling for a different kind of emotional integrity. We may want to restore theatre to the drama-process but we want to exclude, at all costs, the theatrical. We do not want show-biz, simulation or ego-trips. We want art and the challenge of art. And we want that art to penetrate as deeply as it can into both the individual *and* the community.

Fifthly, my account has not described in any detail the differences engendered by the various media, e.g. drama, unlike expressive writing, has a strongly communal and communicative nature from the start. I have consciously emphasised *the similarities* in the process in order to establish the common ground.

Finally, the schema is no more than a schema. It cannot determine the details of teaching. If it reveals an underlying pattern in the arts, teachers must in the creative act of teaching work out what this means for their own expressive discipline. It may provide a general framework, it cannot provide a detailed programme.

VIII

My main intention in this chapter has been to delineate the common ground between the expressive disciplines. I have argued that the arts are not ends in themselves but epistemological tools for the clarification of experience. I am advocating, then, not art for art's sake but for meaning's sake. Art is one of the enduring means for representing (for oneself and for others) those truths latent within our experience, those meanings which are, as it were, curled up inside the seeds of impulse. In exposing the origins of the creative act we found ourselves becoming aware of the bodily sources of art, begun to see art as, in certain ways, the symbolic elaboration of emotional and instinctual energies, an elaboration, however, which always takes place within a society and a culture. Yet it is imperative that we do not slip into the reductive fallacy, of explaining meaning in terms of origins, of confining the nature of art to physiology. Rather we have to cultivate a phenomenological understanding of art-making, seeing it in terms of highly complex human experience and such an approach (briefly adopted in, for example, our study of the English student and Edwin Muir) points to the transformational nature of expressive symbolism. Through art-making and art-responding, we extend our existence. We become more than we could ever have rationally anticipated. Art has its roots in instinct (hence its power) and its blossom in consciousness (hence its educative importance). It is because the expressive disciplines are centrally preoccupied with *the sensuous embodiment of representative meaning* that we refer to them as forming an epistemic community. And once we have made a connection between art and knowledge we can then demonstrate that no school which excludes the arts can be fully involved in the task of educating.

I have also suggested in this chapter that the conception of art developed here, while including the insights of the Progressives, goes well beyond them. We have found ourselves taking their concepts and putting them in a much broader context. While retaining the concept of 'self-expression' we have had to develop the restraining concept of representative form; while wanting to affirm self-realisation we have, at the same time, insisted on collaborative community and cultural heritage. We have struggled to deepen the notion of creative impulse by conferring on it an urge to meaning, an innate desire for reflection, a cognitive disposition. In a similar manner we have taken some of the concepts of the Cambridge School and the Socio-Linguistic School and given them a richer significance. By taking them into another matrix we have given them a further vitality. It has been my aim to describe in the arts a common rhythm, a cumulative sequence moving from self to community back to self in an endless dialectical motion. Our new ground is that of creative mimesis in which the self struggles to become itself within its own culture, dynamically conceived.

To enter the new ground will not be easy. The inexorable technicism of our civilization is against it. So is the utilitarian narrowness of our educational system. So is the ubiquitious mass-packing of symbolism to sell, to entertain, to alternatively soothe and titillate. So is the constricted scientific view of epistemology. So is the general ignorance about the arts. Nothing less than a bold combination of philosophy, pedagogy and politics will do. In this chapter I have concentrated on philosophy and referred to pedagogy. I have tried to make explicit the dynamics of art-making. Following in the tracks of Louis Arnaud Reid, R. G. Collingwood, Herbert Read, Suzanne Langer, Robert Witkin and many others, I have worked to establish a paradigm for the expressive disciplines. In the last chapter I will list some of the changes that such a view necessitates, but I want now to return to English as a literary-expressive subject. I want to make a sketch for the practice of English as an autonomous discipline within the epistemic community of the arts.

3

The Teaching of English as a Literary-Expressive Discipline

I

In the teaching of English as a literary-expressive discipline we are primarily concerned with that practical process through which living impulses are bodied forth in language, related to a deep heritage and transmitted to a responsive community. We are out to nurture that most exacting of all arts, an ability to symbolize within existence, an ability to create forms out of the flow of life in order to enhance existence, or, if not to enhance existence, at least to possess it, to make it our own. One of our major aims is to foster in the individual a symbolic fidelity to emergent experience. It is also our task to see that, wherever fitting, wherever possible, the challenge of authentic art is taken beyond the individual into the imagination of the community. In this we need to understand further the three complementary processes referred to in the last chapter:

(1) The highly personal process through which impulses are amplified, explored and shaped through the expressive medium of language
(2) The cultural process of mimesis through which these impulses are able to find representative forms
(3) The collaborative process of performance and production in which the forms are taken into the community as aesthetic experience and existential challenge.

In this chapter, I will examine these intertwined processes as they relate to the practice of English-teaching as an Expressive Discipline.

II

It seems to me a fault that in our schools, our colleges and universities we invariably present the conclusion of the creative act and seldom examine its origins. Of course, it is necessary to disseminate finished work and struggle for its elucidation and appreciation but we must be careful not to allow the formal architecture of the completed artefact to hide the chaos that may have attended its creation. I suspect that many children and students, half consciously measuring their own powers of thinking and articulating against 'the great work',

the set piece, secretly conclude that their minds function at a completely different level; being messy, spasmodic, confused, idiosyncratic, they decide that *their* thinking/imagining/remembering cannot be worth cultivating. It is as if the intellectual giants think in vast chapters, their interpreters in lucid paragraphs, the teachers in good sentences and the pupils in muddled fragments, dislocated phrases trailing into silence. But this is often (I will not say always) just not the case. To study the origins of significant artefacts is frequently to find their roots in stray notes, floating fragments, in dreams, hunches, images, embodying powerful or obscure or elusive impulses. Indeed this suggests one important approach to the study of literature which is much neglected, namely the examination of a poem in terms of its development, its growth from impulse, through immediate expression, through revision and elaboration to the realization of representative form. Such study can be a liberating experience for students and pupils. For example, I have sometimes taken the following poem by Tony Connor, encouraged in small groups a collaborative interpretation of it and then examined the poet's own account of its slow cumulative development.
The poem by Tony Connor:

HILL-TOP AND GUY FAWKES

Not more than his nose and one eye
was showing. He lurked, as though shy
of being caught looking – like an elderly spinster
behind her curtains when a wedding goes by.

Before we saw him seemed like an age
of fishing becomes shove and nudge;
one of the boys shouted, and there he was poking
slyly dead through the looped-back scum on the lodge.

The police came with iron hooks.
They shooed us off. We made tracks
behind the rusting dump of machinery
and, still as cogs among the little hillocks

of clinker, watched while they dragged him out.
The newspaper said he was seventy-eight,
'of no fixed abode': we played at being vagrants
the rest of the summer holidays, hobbling about

with sacking on our feet, and caps
held out for pennies. Then the shops
began to sell fireworks, and in our fathers cellars
we laboured to build the burnable human shapes.[31]

An account of the genesis of 'Hill-top and Guy Fawkes':

I should perhaps tell you that in the North of England a small reservoir serving a mill – probably a Victorian Cotton Mill or Bleach or Dye Works – is called a 'lodge'.

The ambiguity in question is the possessive 'fathers' in the final verse. Is it singular or plural? To explain the use of it I must go right back to the beginning of the poem. In fact as the origin of this poem is neatly explicable I shall utilize this rare opportunity and tell you how the poem first started in my mind. I worked twelve miles from the large industrial city in which I was born and every day for three years I travelled by diesel train along the man-made squalor of the once pleasant Vale of Irwell. Every day I passed the same lodge with the same scum blown back (by the prevailing wind I suppose) to reveal about half the water's brightness. 'It is like a lace curtain looped back from a shining window', I thought one day in summer. In Autumn I imagined a corpse floating in the water under the scum which I'd already given a name to. It would inevitably be a secretive person peeping forth. 'Who peeps from behind the curtains?' I asked myself. Why, elderly spinsters' 'What at?' Well, things they regret having missed, though they won't admit it. 'Such as?' Weddings, I suppose. 'Is it a spinster, then, in the lodge?' In a way, yes. It's a vagrant, a man who's missed out – unaccommodated man, without a home, without a family. 'Well, to sustain the analogy, what will he be peeping secretly at?' Children enjoying themselves, what else'. By winter – these decisions and ruminations were all very slow – I had remembered the occasion in my childhood when I was indeed present at the dredging of a corpse from a lodge. I knew, simultaneously, that I was making the whole thing up, but the 'memory' was very vivid. It all happened in one of the very few undeveloped areas in our locality – a place called Hill Top. Now it looked as if it was going to be a poem about childhood – childhood and death – but I wasn't clear about anything except the incident of the sighting of the corpse. By this time I was down to the end of the second verse and the law entered naturally, the adult system impinging upon and almost overpowering the vision of children. 'Still as cogs' was a happy simile. Nothing is less still than cogs in use; therefore nothing is stiller than cogs on a rusting dump. The end of the poem arrived as a complete surprise and seemed to possess that autonomous presence that makes one believe – as Coleridge or somebody else that's dead said – that one is merely the midwife at the birth. The playing at vagrants had to take place in the summer holidays, and after that the next big date in the child's year is Bonfire Night and when the effigy of Guy Fawkes is burned. Children playing with death, and then the accurate description of the way in which we built the effigies of Guy Fawkes in the cellars of our houses, out of the way. I remember going down and being frightened (even though I was expecting it) by the giant-sized doll made from old clothes stuffed with newspapers that lolled in one corner amidst the cobwebs. Yet the ear accepts 'our fathers' cellars' in the sense of 'our Father who art in heaven' and the cellars become Hell or the human subconscious in which we labour to build the 'burnable human shapes' – not 'inflammable', which *might* burn, but, burnable, which are intended for burning, acceptable offerings to placate the monster that lusts for us all – Guy Fawkes or the anonymous animals in Auschwitz. The poem, which followed a well-lit if croooked road, suddenly lunges into the dark wood which, almost unnoticed, had been blocking the view on one side since we began.[32]

What is fascinating in Tony Connor's description is the gradual genesis of inner meaning and poetic form out of a mixture of perception, imagination and memory released by the appearance of the lodge's water. It shows how obscure inner meanings can crystallise not in concepts but in imagery. It reveals also how a poet must often engage over a period of time with compelling fragments which initially mean more than he can, at that moment, possibly say.

As English teachers we do well to remind ourselves – and our students – that the creative person learns to accept the smallest offerings, the most ordinary scraps, 'a mound of refuse or the sweepings of a street', as indispensable. He begins to follow without self-consciousness the passing image, the sudden cluster of rhythmically satisfying sounds, the unexpected conjunctions of words, unpredictably rising up from the impulses of his nature. The poet Robert Frost described these offerings as teasles which, he said, he allowed to stick to him until such time as he could make use of them. What seems to me certain is that most forms of education urge the child to neglect the stray and uncertain gifts from the unconscious and that the emphasis on cognitive and abstract knowledge means that these are discarded by nearly all pupils who continue into our sixth forms and into our universities. A student with his intelligence regularly honed, regularly turned to confront the objective universe, will probably not even be aware of such an inner cargo, and if he is aware, because of its confused and enigmatic nature, will tend to dismiss it.

What I am anxious to stress is that creative attending often begins with what is imperfect: with notes, jottings, hints at meaning rather than meaning itself. It is through these fragments that the representative art finally emerges. Through the struggle of building and discarding, creating and destroying – a struggle which may take minutes, hours, weeks, months or years – the writer hopes to attain the animated symmetry of art. I think as English teachers, we should draw attention to the nature of the creative process and to the fact that artefacts are not given like manna from the skies but are made in a concentrated response to what is given in experience or to what rises up from beneath experience. The cry 'only the best' is important but it can give birth prematurely to a hyper-critical attitude and engender in the would-be-creator an impending sense of sterility. And this is unforgivable because it means that many never discover their own powers, never shape their most intimate reflections, never realize the particular rhythm of their own identity, but live solely submerged in the reflections and images of others.

In practical terms, it means that as English teachers we encourage children to live with notes and jottings; we also urge them to work on their work, to revise, to refine and only to present when the piece of writing seems complete. We encourage the habit of first drafts and working copies, of *living with poetry in process*. Those in the sixth form we ask to keep a notebook with ideas, jottings, reflections, which they can draw from in writing and discussion and which helps them to sustain the personal quest for meaning. With young children we allow a large measure of spontaneity but with older children we should provide the tools through which they may become more conscious, more aware of aesthetic form and the evolution of meaning. In particular, perhaps, we should promote the concept of the journal, the discipline of keeping notes which express immediate insights, hunches, difficulties, solutions and contradictions, and which perhaps also houses quotations, cuttings, fragments of conversation, dreams and images. We need to adopt a sober view of inspiration. The revision of work, the acceptance of drafts, the keeping of notes, the habit of the journal, would be the practical outcome. Such an understanding of creative process in literature would also effect our choice of literary texts as well as the way in which we study them in the tutorial, seminar and classroom. Here I find myself in considerable agreement with the writer and teacher Gabriel Josipovici who in an interview suggested:

> Another possibility is to read more of things like writers' diaries and letters. That can help to break down the mystique of the polished and disembodied work and put you in touch with a mind. You get a sense then of the doubt, the hesitations, and the

occasional elations, of someone at work rather than the sort of disembodied confidence of the finished thing. This would be true of Lawrence's letters for example – or may be there's a case for setting Keats' letters for 'A' level study and leaving the poems for optional reading if you're interested. I'm thinking here of something quite different of course from using biographical knowledge to explicate a text.[33]

We have to encourage our students and pupils to sense the existential source of art-making, the underlying quest for meaning rooted in the body's impulses and moving outwards in search of reflection and representative utterance.

The ability to know little in order that one may know more later; the ability to be creatively involved in what is immediately given so that one may shape it further: the ability to slowly transform life through honest and alert symbolization: these I would say are some of the abilities we should be trying to cultivate as teachers of English. They contrast dramatically with many of the aims now set for teachers and lecturers. Pupils and students are forever encouraged to think *outside* their existence, solving problems, imposing abstract schemata upon the world in a way which leaves their feelings and their relationships to that world untouched, unexplored and uneducated. In this sense, much of education still constitutes a flight from existence and represents, in Kierkegaard's words, 'the victory of abstraction over the individual'. Alongside discursive linear logic developed in the humanities and sciences, we must assert the value of poetic, imagistic and associative logic – the logic of feeling and imagination and seek to develop it in all the expressive disciplines. This calls for a new kind of arts pedagogy in English teaching.

Our understanding of the first stages of art-making calls for teaching methods which encourage in the students a willingness to take risks, in which critical judgements are kept to a minimum, in which the expressive medium is explored and its possibilities personally tested. Words are tried out by the student for fit and, as self-expression moves towards representative expression, many may well be discarded. At this stage in the art-making process the teacher of English has to promote that 'momentary and passing madness' which Schiller claimed was 'found in all real creators'. In this madness Schiller declared the intellect 'had withdrawn its watchers from the gates, and the ideas rush in pell-mell, and only then does it review and inspect the multitude'. Thus, as I have argued, we need to give space for rough drafts, for work in process, for the securing of the molten raw material before the gradual refining of it. Transferring our methods to literary studies, we need, at times, to sympathetically examine the genesis of poems, stories and novels and impart to our students through the reading of letters, autobiography and journals a keener awareness of how the art-maker works his medium to create the animated and representative forms of human experience.

III

I have emphasised the messy nature of the creative process, but this process does not happen outside the boundaries set by inherited culture. As was argued in the last chapter the language in which we struggle to forge our personal meanings is the language we have learnt by imitating others; the forms in which we seek to recreate our experience are, invariably, the forms that have been made availabe by our traditions. *There is no creation outside symbolism and the many modes of symbolising experience we have learnt (or failed to learn) through a prolonged and not uncreative process of mimesis.* It is thus a quite understandable paradox that many of the most original men have imitated their great predecessors and have only slowly and painfully surpassed that which they imitated. It is not altogether different in the classroom where we will find children's own writing taking in a line from Lawrence, an echo from Ted Hughes, an image from a Chinese poem. This is the way in which all culture is assimilated and the way in which we come to our thoughts, beliefs, and, indeed, our very identities. Here we encounter a recurring paradox. The more we are immersed in the vital symbolic forms of a culture the more free we can become; the more language we possess the greater the possibilities for differentiated and sensitive perception, feeling and thinking. The child/pupil/student has to struggle to find his voice within the culture, within the language. He achieves this through the act of creative mimesis, through which he absorbs into himself the inherited symbols and in turn begins to use them in his own personal way for the elucidation and celebration of his own experience. There is nothing esoteric about creative mimesis – it is the underlying pattern of all growth, the tireless dynamic behind cultural transformation.

With· the concept of creative mimesis I want now to turn my attention to the introduction of literary forms and structures in the teaching of English. Through experimenting with a variety of literary forms the pupil becomes more deeply acquainted with the medium within which, as we have seen, he struggles to represent his experience. The more power he has over the medium the greater the chances for symbolically rendering the informing impulse. I am not advocating an uncritical return to the reproduction of model passages so widely practiced at the beginning of this century. Yet this practice, deriving from Renaissance and Greek education, possessed a certain wisdom which has been overlooked. As G. H. Bantock has pointed out 'the purpose was to encourage a high degree of internalization of the best writing so that the grasp acquired could then be redeployed in "free composition".' In this way the individual found his voice within the culture (a voice, in fact, can only exist because of a culture) though not necessarily in agreement with it. The Progressive School of English in elevating the individual tended to overlook the liberating potential of received symbolic forms. As a result of its influence art contracted to 'self-expression'. At worst it became little more than an autistic scream, a barbaric yelp, a defiant belch. And yet, as Collingwood pointed out so succinctly in *The Principles of Art*:

> If an artist may say nothing except what he has invented by his own sole efforts, it stands to reason he will be poor in ideas. If he could take what he wants wherever he could find it, as Euripedes and Dante and Michelangelo and Shakespeare and Bach were free, his larder would always be full, and his cookery might be worth tasting.[34]

A comment by Dylan Thomas on the development of his own poetry confirms Collingwood's defence of mimesis:

> I bulldozed through print . . . I stomped pun-shod and neigh-nonnied in a nosebag of adjectives. I had to imitate and parody, consciously and unconsciously: I had to try to learn what made words tick, beat, blaze, because I wanted to write what I wanted to write before I knew how to write or what I wanted to.[35]

If, as I have claimed throughout this book, we are to take the impulse into the culture, we must make the archetypal metaphors and the inherited repertoire of forms available to the student. If we are to issue a request for creative exploration we must not withold the means for its realization.

In *The Teaching of English in Schools 1900–1970* David Shayer describes a textbook entitled *Matter, Form and Style* which was written by Hardress O'Grady and which emerged out of the classical tradition of imitation. According to Shayer the manual, published in 1912, adopted:

> a craft, practical approach to writing. The pupil is taken not through clause analysis, parsing, figures of speech and sentence construction but through a study of various styles of writing (descriptive, emotive, satiric, persuasive) based on (1) his own attempts in these styles, (2) the reading of good examples taken from professionals. O'Grady presents his pupils with prose passages which they must read and compare for effectiveness of presentation, trying their own hand at the technique (including short stories) with a list of good follow up assignments. The book is extremely important because it rejects the wretched grammar-composition link, and insists that writing is learnt by writing and that the best way to proceed is to manoeuvre pupils into the writing situation first and show them what they are doing (in stylistic and not grammatical terms) afterwards.[36]

Although there may be little comprehension of the phases of art-making, there is, I contend, a methodological soundness in O'Grady's approach. If the forms of writing mentioned are inadequate yet there is a bringing together of literature, writing and criticism – the activities so central to English as an expressive discipline. There is also an awareness of the need for excellent examples to guide the student in his own writing. As I have indicated the need for examples, of model passages, has not been emphasised enough in the teaching of expressive writing and is one of the reasons why so many teachers, with partial justification, associate 'creative writing' with verbal excess and emotional slovenliness. In fact, we stand in need of a good primer much like Ezra Pound's *ABC of Reading* only written for classroom use, showing the work of young writers, introducing the various prose and poetry forms as well as a certain critical vocabulary and, above all, generating a feel for the power and urgency of the creative word. Ted Hughes' *Listening and Writing* is working in the right direction but it isn't sufficiently comprehensive.

As English teachers we can consciously introduce different forms for our students and pupils to experiment with and internalize. These forms are powerful in that they release new energy and suggest ways in which the primary material of individual experience can be shaped. The emphasis on 'total originality' in our society has become absurd. Even if such originality could exist, it would not be understood. In the living symbol, the self and the community, the present and the past, the new and the inherited, meet. We stress both the creative process and the presentation of symbolic structure because it is just this sort of meeting we are hoping to achieve in the classroom.

Let me give two examples of creative mimesis taken from a first year class at a comprehensive school. The English teacher has read a selection of primitive poems about animals and then invited the class to write about an animal or insect of which they have some knowledge. One of the primitive poems is as follows:

THE LOCUST

What is a locust?
Its head, a grain of corn; its neck, the hinge of a knife;
Its horns, a bit of thread, its chest is smooth and burnished;
Its body is like a knife-handle;
Its hock, a saw; its spittle, ink;
Its underwings, clothing for the dead.
On the ground – it is like the clouds.
Approaching the ground, it is rain glittering in the sun;
Lighting on a plant, it becomes a pair of scissors;
Walking it becomes a razor,
Desolation walks with it.

a poem written by one of the children is on a spider:

WHAT IS A SPIDER?

Her web: a death trap
Her head: a berry of night shade
Her body: a ball of black cloth
Her legs: grasping prongs of steel
Her eyes: blots of ink alert and glaring!

She lures her prey into her deadly trap
Once in her grasp she devours them greedily!

Victoria Ross

It is clear that the structure of the primitive poem is being imitated. It is also fairly clear that some of the imagery has been unconsciously assimilated and recast; in 'The locust' the spittle is ink, in the spider poem the eyes are 'blots of ink alert and glaring; in 'The locust' the wings are 'clothing for the dead', in the child's poem, the body is 'a ball of black cloth'. But this is not passive imitation, it is more a form of creative mimesis. The child is simultaneously imitating and transforming. The structure and imagery of the poem are providing an effective way for her to mediate her own experience.

My second example comes from the same lesson. One of the other primitive poems read by the teacher was 'Leopard':

LEOPARD

Gentle hunter
his tail plays on the ground
while he crushes the skull.

Beautiful death
who puts on a spotted robe
when he goes to his victim.

Playful killer
whose loving embrace
splits the antelope's heart.

It is, I think, a marvellously concentrated metaphysical poem. Again, it is clear
that the following poem written after listening to it has, in some way, emerged out
of it.

THE THRUSH

The thrush is a beautiful bird
Wearing a spotted robe
Proudly he holds his head up high
Listening to a far off sound.

The thrush is a hungry bird
With an ever watchful eye
Waiting for the innocent snail
To come crawling slowly by
Snatching it as quick as lightning.

He smashes his victim against a stone
To crack its hard shell
Tap, tap, tap like a hammer
Striking a nail
Then pecks out the soft body of the snail.

Iain Heather

In the child's poem we cannot but hear the echoes: the spotted robe, the victim,
the contrasts between hardness and softness; yet, at the same time, we recognize a
new voice. The poem on the thrush stands in it own right but we know it could not
have existed had not 'Leopard' been there, embodying a particular pattern of
symbolization. (Even the three stanza structure is possibly an unconscious
imitation of the primitive poem). Essential features of the original primitive
poems have been internalized by the children and re-used as a means of exploring
their own experiences. Voices emerging from voices. Creative mimesis.

I want now to look briefly at the initiation into poetic forms. I believe that the
teacher, with due consideration for the class in question, can set quite specific
forms with which children can experiment. In an article appropriately entitled
'Making poems' the English teacher Neil Powell describes and reflects upon a
lesson in which he had set his mixed-ability fourth year to write a villanelle:

> That is why if one is to teach people how to make poems at all, I think one should
> start with the fascination of what is difficult – the forms, the structures, the skills.
> The first poem I remember writing at school which gave me real satisfaction
> (enough for me to have preserved a copy) was a villanelle. I'd come across one in an
> anthology – it was Empson's 'Missing Dates' – and, though unable to make much
> sense of the thing, I recently asked my Group IV class to write a villanelle each for
> an assignment (I gave them the option of a sonnet if they were really stuck). One of
> my colleagues set the same assignment for her part of the group; another colleague,
> Peter Scupham, wrote a villanelle for the occasion and I polished up an unfinished one
> of my own; then we showed these to our groups, together with villanelles by Auden
> and Dylan Thomas, though not the rather gnarled Empson. I explained the rules of

the game briefly, but suggested that a close study of the examples was the best approach. The class contains some who are having one-to-one remedial English coaching and a couple who may be reading English at Oxbridge in three or four years' time – a wide range. I'd guess that about half of them found the exercise rewarding and surprising, while perhaps half a dozen produced unmistakably well-made, successful poems. That is as good a result as I could have expected from a comprehension or an essay assignment. Next time, they will try a sestina.[37]

It is to be noted how the selection of excellent examples is used to focus and make possible the work. It is also of pedagogic importance that both the teachers write and present their own villanelles, not, presumably to impress the class but to demonstrate that the writing of poetry can be in mature life an essential, an engaging and an exacting pursuit. Villanelles are introduced to promote the writing of villanelles with, in the judgement of the teacher, considerable success. One of my English students, suddenly preoccupied with the power of images in poetry, took into her mixed-ability fourth year group one or two Imagist poems including Ezra Pound's *Metro-station*. Faithfully following the simple structure of Pound's poem, where a concept is given then converted into an image, she suggested that the class jot down their visual responses to a list of objects: life, death, depression, the wind, people, etc. She received the following imagist poems in response:

People
    like pools of murky,
        mysterious water.

The winters rough sea like a
        cracked mirror

The young bride
    like a silver birch in the
        dark wood.

Life,
    like a cloud of deceit, sin
        and untruth.

Death, like eternal darkness, a
    tunnel running away from
        the light.

Her hair flowed from her head like
    sand-dunes in a desert.

Some of these images are highly evocative yet they have been released in the imagination through the use of a simple and formal structure. Indeed the following poem, released on another occasion by the same kind of work, shows a most sensitive imitation of Ezra Pound's 'Metro-station':

The apparition of bees around a flower
Freckles on a pale skinned child.

Subsequent work with such a class could possibly include a closer study of the imagist movement (taking some of the earlier poems of Ezra Pound, T. E. Hulme and T. S. Eliot) and an invitation to the pupils to develop a longer poem out of a single image: perhaps also some work on haiku with its more formal demands.

As I have written extensively on the initiation of the child into the heritage of poetic forms in *Root and blossom*, I will merely list the techniques which can be introduced. These are some of the main poetic forms:

(1) Free verse
(2) Imagist poems
(3) Riddles
(4) Shape poems
(5) Typographical poems
(6) Parallelism and Repetition
(7) Songs
(8) Ballads
(9) Haiku
(10) Blank Verse
(11) Sonnets
(12) Villanelles
(13) Sestinas
(14) Heroic Couplets

Forms in prose, of equal importance, could be listed as follows:

(1) Simple sketches relating to (*a*) mood
                                (*b*) place
                                (*c*) character
(2) Fables
(3) Parables
(4) Stories ⎫ (these forms would require practice in (*a*) dialogue,
(5) Novelettes ⎬ (*b*) character, (*c*) narrative, (*d*) use of symbol, (*e*) ways of
(6) Novels ⎭ penetrating into the subjective life of the characters.)

Various forms of essay writing need presenting and developing, e.g.

(1) Essays in persuasion
(2) Essays in interpretation
(3) Essays in biography
(4) Satirical sketches

The various forms of written drama should also be explored, e.g.

(1) Short dramatic sketches: tragedy/comedy etc.
(2) One act plays
(3) Play for voices (as if for radio)
(4) Full length plays – (*a*) for stage
                               (*b*) for TV
                               (*c*) for radio
(5) Film scripts
(6) Documentaries

Finally, I think, there is an important place for the more introspective and personal forms of writing, e.g.

(1) The journal
(2) The diary
(3) Autobiography

The effective introduction of all these forms, I have suggested, requires that the teacher finds excellent models – examples where the form is superbly consistent with itself and the content not too far removed from what the particular class in question can be expected to grasp or imagine. It also requires that he releases an expressive impulse in the student. Forms, if they are to be creatively used rather than mechanically emulated, must be taken down into the deeper forces of art-making. An emphasis on poetic and literary forms has to be complemented by an emphasis on originating impulse and creative process. Without such a dialectic, 'personal' writing can easily become diffuse and aimless, while 'formal' writing can deteriorate to the level of mere technique, of clever simulation and bad rhetoric. Our aim must always be to keep the received symbolism of the culture close to the sources of individual creativity. The two principles could be defined as follows:

(1) Subjective being can only find itself through cultural forms.
(2) Cultural forms are kept alive through the subjective quest for wholeness of being.

There is also a third principle which is related and corrective. At the beginning of the chapter I described this principle as the collaborative process of performance and production through which what has been well made is taken into the community as aesthetic experience and existential challenge. In chapter 2 it was presented as the last two phases of art-making. However, before drawing this principle into our argument I would like to translate theory into practice and show how writing can be developed in the classroom and workshop. I will take examples from my own work with a group of PGCE students on a course which I will describe more fully in the next chapter. Perhaps I should also point out that the conception of the five phases of the art-making process evolved out of just such practical workshops.

IV

I will describe in the barest outlines three sessions with a group of PGCE English students, sessions intended to provide a metaphor for how to work in the classroom.

SESSION ONE: FROM EXPRESSIVE IMPULSE TO REPRESENTATIVE FORM

Without introduction and without warning I hand out to each of the sixteen students the two photographs of the Grauballe Man reproduced here:
I ask for complete silence and urge the students to contemplate the images and

to list, without inhibition, all their immediate impressions, feelings and associations. I allow this five minutes of time. Here is a characteristic list:

Dead body
Decay
Like tree roots
Isolated
Exposed
Frightens (me)
Something vegetable like in the shapes, texture, cabbage
Field of cabbages — rotting –
Merging into the ground
Ends of arms are becoming one with the earth
Furrowed field in the background
Egyptian mummy – swaddled – Rousseau and restriction of baby
Hand becoming one with the earth
Human – what does that mean – how is it different from world
Finger nails – baby's nails – monkey's nails – always surprise me – They surprise me here
End of arms are becoming one with the earth
curved shape of ribs like the side of a boat
Leg musculature like picture in one of John's books of the Anatomy Lesson
Strange appearance of the breast-like tendrils of plants
Makes me feel desolate
Is it male or female
greek

I then ask the students to look at their lists to see if they can sense an emerging pattern, some unifying thread which runs through the initial response. I suggest that they now view the rough jottings as the raw material for a more developed piece of writing. Twenty minutes is given to this.

Here is how the student worked on the list given above.

Desolate
exposed once-living Thing
A cabbage rotting in the field
Textured to oneness with the soil
Root creature, furrowed into peace
The human
The baby's nails always surprise me so—
    So new a
Complete, and fully finished
    at the hour of death
In dissolution, one thing last to go.

Finally I ask that the more developed version is taken to some kind of completion. The following poem derived from the jottings above:

ASSOCIATIONS

Desolate, exposed, once-living thing,
Man-tendrils, rotting in the field,
Textured to oneness with the soil,
Root-creature, furrowed into peace.

A baby's nails always surprise me so,
Complete, perfect, at the hour of birth!
Buffered and filed for adult vanity,
In dissolution, are nails the last to go?

Swaddled no longer is the newborn child
But Death, behind the times, still binds the corpse
(An earth-wrapped, rigid parody of life)
Before permitting slow release from form.

The structure of such a workshop takes the student through the first three phases of art-making, from impulse to working within a medium, from free approximate self expression to the possible realization of representative form. The session can be viewed as an exercise to initiate the students into art-making. In opening sessions I think that time-counts can actually serve a creative purpose. They provoke a sense of urgency which can overcome the self-critical inhibiting tendencies.

As this was the students' very first writing workshop I did not take the art-making into the second movement of presentation and evaluation. Instead I introduced Seamus Heaney's 'The Grauballe man' which had been written in response to the same photographs. In this way I was implicitly linking the art-making of my students with the art-making within the culture. The point was not necessarily to make comparisons but to sense the common task of creating out of, in this case, shocked and engaged impulses in response to the photographs.

THE GRAUBALLE MAN

As if he had been poured
in tar, he lies
on a pillow of turf
and seems to weep

the black river of himself.
The grain of his wrists
is like bog oak,
the ball of his heel

like a basalt egg.
His instep has shrunk
cold as a swan's foot
or a wet swamp root.

His hips are the ridge
and purse of a mussel,
his spine an eel arrested
under a glisten of mud.

The head lifts,
the chin is a visor
raised above the vent
of his slashed throat

that has tanned and toughened.
The cured wound
opens inwards to a dark
elderberry place.

Who will say 'corpse'
to his vivid cast?
Who will say 'body'
to his opaque repose?

And his rusted hair,
a mat unlikely
as a foetus's.
I first saw his twisted face

in a photograph,
a head and shoulder
out of the peat,
bruised like a forceps baby

but now he lies
perfected in my memory,
down to the red horn
of his nails,

hung in the scales
with beauty and atrocity:
with the Dying Gaul
too strictly compassed

on his shield,
with the actual weight
of each hooded victim,
slashed and dumped.[38]

SESSION TWO: INTRODUCING A POETIC FORM: AN EXAMPLE OF CREATIVE MIMESIS

In this session the impulse for writing is all but generated by the medium itself. I begin by asking the students to jot down their associations to such words as:
night
moon
snow
winter
rush-hour
marriage
tidal wave
death
rose.

I then hand each student a different atmospheric picture. I ask them to make a further list of associations in response to the image. When this is completed I introduce the haiku form. I read some examples, talk briefly about its development, indicate its simple structure (three lines: first line, five syllables; second line, seven syllables; third line, five syllables). The students are then asked to look at their various word and picture associations and to develop them within the structure of the haiku.

At the end of the workshop there is a group presentation of the haiku. Here are some examples from the work produced:

October exhales
Its deadly wood smoke odours
Upon the furrow

———

Eternal love vows
Ceremonial facade
Dressed in altar white

———

An ageing stubble
Guttered man plays tuneless song
Spoon on rusted tin

———

Russet brambly leaves
They know the art of dying
I just travel on

The aim of the workshop was not to present a form as an isolated exercise, but to bring a form to bear upon personally felt responses which had been released by the free word and picture associations. The cultural form is brought as an expressive possibility to the emerging experience. The workshop is an example of creative mimesis, the meeting of individual impulse and received symbolic form. The haiku would seem to be a highly accessible form for this kind of writing at all levels of work.

SESSION THREE: IMPULSE – FIRST VERSIONS – PRESENTATION AND EVALUATION – REALIZATION OF FINAL FORM

In this session, after a reading of some primitive poems, I asked the students to imaginatively identify with any elemental force: wind, wave, fire, frost, thunder: to identify with the force and to allow it to speak through them.

I want to show here the development of one piece of writing through a series of approximations until it attained representative form. One of the influences on the final form was an English workshop in which the piece in its third draft was presented to and evaluated by the English group. It will be seen how such practical criticism can work as a refining agent in the creative process.

This was the very first draft of Pauline's poem on Fire:

I start harmless, unnoticeable,
A flicker a crack then oh,

I must eat, oh my appetite consumes me
So I spread, emerging furtively at first
Lest my prey should

My beginning is an accident
I am a surprise to myself, I
Put out my feelers, a curling flicker
a crackle, woh, wave of hunger consumes me
I emerge and spread and as I spread I devour
and as I devour, I multiply
So that more must I swallow
My quivering tentacles blindly reach
up and out for supporting
surfaces, embracing and disintegrating the
life source of the old oak

   I feed on dry matter but my
hunger is never satisfied and I must
look to the living I snarl at
the damp, splutter, but I shall conquer
For I must destroy to live, I
speed of my motion terrifies
me as the intensity of my hunger
My path is erratic and blind and scarey
My contact is violent, painful, deadly
Earth, water, air

warmth
   life-giving warmth
      Earth feeds me, wind inspirits me
involuntary hunger
a dancer a ravager
a teaser a murderer
Rage
I terrify myself my controlled brother
ember

In the second draft (see below) there is an attempt to shape further this primary material. The opening idea is kept but rephrased more succinctly as:

   I begin as an accident.
   I have no time to consider
      the surprise of my being.

There is also an attempt to terminate the passage, not to let it go on aimlessly – but this the reader will notice is changed again, and with greater success in the third draft.

SECOND DRAFT COPY

I begin as an accident. I have no time to consider the surprise of my being. My (illusive) feelers begin to creep involuntarily before there is time to arrest or order. I am teased forward, the dance ripples, through me, the motion impels me. Wind inspirits me, lifting me & flinging me into flickering diffusion. My essence clings to the ground as my tongue worms hungrily nervously gripped by a consuming, convulsive hunger, I *must* devour, as I devour I spread lightning speed. My quivering tentacles reach wildly up and out for surfaces to embrace, to cremate Earth feeds me. The speed of my growth, the intensity of my appetite terrifies me. My being flares in a raging, roaring heat. I shan't dance, I shall ravage, I shan't tease, I shall murder, I 't at the damp, splutter but I shall conquer For I must destroy to LIVE

The third copy below was the final copy until the group workshop in criticism:

I AM   Pauline Down.

     I begin, an accident. I have no time to consider the surprise of my being. My illusive feelers begin to tease, to creep forward before there is time to arrest, to order. I am urged into play. The dance ripples through me, the motion impels me. Wind inspirits me, lifting me, flinging me into flickering diffusion. My essence clings to the ground as my tongues worm nervously: gripped suddenly by a consuming hunger, I must devour. Convulsively, my quivering tentacles reach wildly up and out for surfaces to embrace, dry matter to cremate. They snarl at the damp, spit and master. I devour and spread and devour and devour. Earth feeds me. My being flares into a raging, roaring heat. No longer dancing, I ravage; no longer teasing, I murder. For I must destroy to live! The intensity of my appetite, the speed of my growth terrifies me. WHERE WILL IT ALL END?
. . . . .at water.

     In the practical criticism workshop all the writing produced was duplicated read out and evaluated. Pauline's piece received some praise but it was felt that, at points, words were being used too indulgently, e.g. 'convulsively, my quivering tentacles reach wildly up and out for surfaces to embrace' would be better simply as 'convulsively my tentacles reach up', for, it was pointed out, convulsive includes within it both the feeling of 'quivering' and 'wildly'. The power of economy in language was stressed. And it was also thought that the prose passage might move more fluently and tellingly in a form of free verse. Pauline considered these suggestions and the final(?) piece kept in her file was as follows:

I AM

I begin
An accident,
I have no time to consider
The surprise of my being,
My elusive feelers begin to tease,
To creep forward before there is time to arrest,
To order.

I am urged into play
The dance ripples through me, the motion impels me
Wind inspirits me!
Lifting me, flinging me into flickering diffusion.

I cling to the ground
As my tongues work nervously:
Gripped suddenly by a consuming hunger
I must devour!
Convulsively my tentacles reach up, reach out

For surfaces to embrace
Dry matter to cremate
They snarl at the damp
Spit and master

I devour and spread and devour and devour
Earth feeds me;
My being flares into a raging, roaring heat
No longer dancing,
I ravage
No longer teasing,
I murder
For I must destroy to live!
The intensity of my appetite, the speed of my growth
Terrifies me!
WHERE WILL IT ALL END
. . . .
. . . . at water

Pauline's poem, like the other poems quoted in this section, have been selected to illustrate the art-making process as it unfolds in English studies. They are offered as simple examples of creative mimesis, of living with poetry in process, and of the slow uncertain movement of working from notes and fragments towards representative utterance. They are intended to suggest a pattern and a teaching technique both of which will be described more fully in the next chapter. The comments below give some indication as to what the students made of the workshops and of how they related them to their own teaching practice:

REFLECTIONS ON THE WRITING WORKSHOPS

I found the workshops at the beginning of the course valuable from an academic and personal point of view. It seemed most odd to produce creative work to the hands of a clock and be one of a large group of creators confined to a small space all writing about the same pictures. It took some time to sink into my mind that that is what we often ask teenagers to do without any consideration of their feelings or position at all. A teacher is usually primarily concerned with the work produced at the end of forty-five minutes rather than the conditions of the process. My biggest fear was that of judgement. I couldn't really cope with the idea of my personal creation being judged, probably in comparison with those of the rest of the group. Peter stressed to us that the value of the work we produced was of no real consequence; the process and the conditions which we experience were to be noted first. I remember being agonised and confused at first because I didn't really understand what we had to do. Peter talked about jotting down words and images from the pictures and forming them into some kind of written piece. This seemed so vague. I felt I needed him to say 'write a poem' or 'write a description' or something equally constraining; something which would set limits for me to work within. At first I didn't really consider the limits we were already working within. Afterwards I noted in my course diary 'Laying aside the product – which in my case was not particularly worth considering – I found the process stimulating'. Why did I find it stimulating? I think I began to realise for myself what I intended to ask my pupils to do in a lesson. It would have helped if we could have looked more closely (and anonymously) at what the group had produced. Were people actually producing something worthwhile or were they a collection of desperate nonsequitors produced in order to show that we were capable of writing something down.

When Peter imposed further constraints on us and asked us to write some Haiku on individual pictures and paintings, we all saw the results which were quite impressive. We enjoyed writing under such strict and limited conditions.

It is difficult really to measure the relevance of these workshops to our own teaching. In my own experience in the school I have been certainly more aware of what I have been asking the children to do. It has also made me aware of wider possibilities in the classroom. Julian and I both take sixth form poetry appreciation classes. We have been rather disappointed that their approach to poetry is so negative and blasé. We wondered how we could somehow give them a fresh glimpse of understanding poetry. In one lesson we gave them a xeroxed picture and made them go through the same process we had endured in the workshops. With the exception of one or two, none had written anything before except much lower down the school. The results were extremely good; in half an hour each one has produced a piece of sensitive and coherent writing. The workshops have made me somehow more moral about the decisions I take when I plan a lesson. What am I actually trying to get these children to do? Am I being reasonable and fair? How can I get them to put thoughts and words together so that they have, as Ted Hughes says, some kind of 'spirit', and not produce lifeless clichés which take no-one any further on? I am not sure that we have had enough of these workshops to clarify our own thoughts on all this. I feel that lights have been switched on here and there in my mind but haven't really illuminated everything fully. Perhaps they are not meant to, and anyway, this term has only been a beginning.

Nicolette Winton

When we realised on our first Thursday afternoon that we were actually being asked to write creatively, most of us looked at each other in anxious amazement. I, for one, had not written anything except a diary (and that bastion of English literature the critical essay) since the fifth form at school. No-one had asked me to write anything after 'O' Level English Language, and knowing that I would never become a poet, novelist or playwright, I did not see the point in writing merely for my own amusement. When I met my husband I gave up writing my diary. I felt it had served its purpose of being a sort of father-confessor during my adolescent years, so I put it away with other childish things.

Thus, if I could have avoided creative writing on Thursdays I would have done! Now, however, I am very pleased that I didn't avoid it. Apart from its value to me as an individual, its relevance to the teaching of English cannot be denied. Firstly, it has made me realise and understand the difficulties faced by pupils when asked to write creatively (especially in less than perfect conditions and under pressure of time or from the teacher). Secondly, it has made me think about the process of creative writing and how it may be made to work in the classroom.

For example, in our first session, we discussed a poem 'Hill-top and Guy Fawkes' by Tony Connor and then read the poet's own notes on the writing of that poem. From this we concluded that poems do not appear on the page as if by magic, but in fact begin with an image or vague idea and develop, often through many stages and as many weeks or months into the final, finished artefact. We put this into practice ourselves, in the first sessions, by responding tentatively to pictures. My responses were in the form of questions, and rough notes which were then formed into a poem. We used the same groping process in our next two sessions, leading to autobiographical pieces and Haiku poems. In both cases what seemed an impossible task became possible through this method of an immediate tentative response to a stimulus followed by expansion and revision.

All this has greatly influenced my teaching. In my own school life, compositions were written in response to a title on the board. The title was presumably meant to be the key to a gate which when unlocked would release a flood of imaginative ideas. Now, I would never ask anyone to write creatively without providing a stimulus such as a picture, poem, story or dramatic experience, nor would I expect anyone to write a poem or story straight into his best book without revision. I always try to work in stages with the children gradually leading them towards a poem or story.

However, I should add that even this method has its problems. Some children object to the intermediate stages and want to know why they can't get on with writing their poems instead of 'wasting all this time'. I have also been told that there have been complaints about the second-year children writing too many poems when they can't even write sentences yet (not necessarily my second years). And some of my children do not enjoy creative writing at all.

Claire Armstrong

V

There is a marked tendency in our educational establishments to see written work as an all but confidential transaction between the student and the teacher. Essays are written for the teacher, commented on by the teacher and returned by the teacher. It is not, generally, different with the writing of stories, poems and reviews. Somehow a wider context which might give the writing a further audience and a further significance is missing. It is as if all his life the teacher is preparing his student for that private moment when in silence and enforced isolation he will have to write for some remote examiner in the hope that he has managed to choose what the inscrutable judge is looking for and so secure the certificate which he needs for quite other purposes. The examination system is a perfect image of cerebral abstraction and alienation. It confers an authority on patterns of evaluation which are, on educational grounds, hopelessly inadequate and does much to prevent our schools from becoming true collaborative centres of making and learning.

That the characteristic pattern of evaluation is as I have described it was confirmed by the Schools Council Project *Writing and Learning Across the Curriculum.* In that study, the researchers divided the concept of audience into six different categories: self, trusted adult, pupil-teacher dialogue, teacher examiner, peer group and the public. The following diagrams disclose, through an analysis of scripts across 300 secondary schools, the limited audiences which pupils actually address in their writing tasks:

AUDIENCE BY YEAR (percentages of year sample)

	Year 1	Year 3	Year 5	Year 7
Self	0	0	0	0
Trusted adult	2	3	2	1
Pupil-teacher dialogue	51	45	36	19
Teacher examiner	40	45	52	61
Peer group	0	0	0	0
Public	0	1	5	6
Miscellaneous (translation, dictation, exercises etc.)	7	6	5	13

AUDIENCE BY SUBJECT (percentages of subject sample)

	English	History	Geography	RE	Science
Self*	0	0	0	0	0
Trusted adult	5	0	0	5	0
Pupil-teacher dialogue	65	17	13	64	7
Teacher examiner	18	69	81	22	87
Peer group	0	0	0	0	0
Public	6	0	0	0	0
Miscellaneous	6	14	6	10	6

*(The team considered that in any involved writing the self was a significant part of the writer's sense of audience. They therefore defined the category for their purposes as covering items obviously unconnected with an audience – rough work for instance.)

The reader can observe how nearly all the writing is confined to the single audience of teacher, either in his capacity as commentator or as marker. The solitary and the communal, the individual writing for his own satisfaction and the individual writing for an actual community, both are all but completely neglected. Behind this practice lies the formidable power of the examination system and, behind that, an utterly outmoded disembodied notion of pure objective knowledge. In fact, the chart tells us more about the pathologies of our schools and our culture than about the true meaning of educational activity. It is true, that to a certain extent, the arts have been able to resist the dominant pattern of presentation and evaluation. In particular, drama in our schools has established an alternative pattern of communal making and collaborative evaluation, with the teacher working as fellow-artist and experienced guide rather than exclusive judge. Drama has not been corrupted by false expectations and philosophical misconceptions in the way English has. And the English teacher, therefore, has much to learn from this discipline. The challenge on the English teacher is to turn his classroom into a busy workshop, to enter it as a practitioner and to promote, wherever fitting, collaborative methods of evaluation and production. In general, the class as a whole should form the community for the writing produced by the pupils, and, beyond that, the school, and, beyond that, the surrounding community.

In the second chapter it was argued that within art-making itself there was a communicative thrust, that, to the extent that the art-maker felt he had achieved representative form, there was a proportionate desire to show the work to others. This communicative intention has to be satisfied if art-work is to remain vital and meaningful. As Collingwood put it in *The Principles of Art*:

> Unless he (the art-maker) sees his own proclamation, 'This is good', echoed on the faces of his audience – 'Yes, that is good' – he wonders whether he was speaking the truth or not. He thought he had enjoyed and recorded a genuine aesthetic experience, but has he? Was he suffering from a corruption of consciousness? Has his audience judged him better than he judged himself?[40]

Thus the audience, providing it is alert and serious, serves a quite indispensable collaborative function. In the workshop I described earlier in which Pauline's poem was read out and discussed, the suggestions by the English students and myself, lead to a considerable improvement in the organization of the writing. Revision, in response to a reader's criticism, is a common occurrence in literature; one thinks for example of Ezra Pound's influence on *The Waste Land*. A sensitive audience becomes all but a necessary condition for the development of style, the slow emergence of a distinct voice within the culture. One of the most difficult tasks of the English teacher is to delicately create in the classroom, school and community such a responsive audience.

How can it be done? It requires that the English teacher consider more carefully the last two phases of the creative process in which, as we have said, the art-work is taken out into the community as aesthetic experience and existential challenge. It requires that the communal nature of art is also given its due emphasis, that the whole school is envisaged as the place for display, enactment, ritual, presentation and celebration. More specifically, I would like to make five practical suggestions.

Firstly, I suggest that the English teacher holds fairly regular workshops in practical criticism where the work of the pupils, with their permission, is duplicated, read out, discussed and evaluated. The workshop should give sensitive attention both to the reading out of the writing (different ways of reading indicating different ways of interpreting the work) and to the practical ways in which the writing might be developed (which, of course, the writer must always be free to reject). Sometimes the work of other writers can be taken; sometimes, perhaps, the work of the teacher. I have concentrated on poetic writing in this chapter but the practical criticism workshop should embrace all kinds of expressive writing: novels, stories, reviews, essays, plays, documentaries, film-scripts, etc.

Secondly, I suggest that the English department is committed to publishing; that it occasionally publishes some of the best individual writers in the school in attractive individual volumes; that it also publishes, in conjunction with the art department, a regular journal in which wide selection of art-work and written-work is well reproduced; that teachers, as a matter of course, are expected to contribute; that pupils are actively engaged in the running and organizing of the publishing; and that adult writers in the community are also brought into the publishing programme. The advent of comparatively cheap photo-litho printing has made this proposal wholly practical.

Thirdly, I suggest that frequent readings are arranged. The oral energy of poetry – the potency of the spoken word – has been badly neglected. Readings from pupils' original writing could be a regular feature of one assembly each week. Readings, perhaps based on the published volumes, could also be arranged in the local community – in the library, for example – and in the school on public occasions.

Fourthly, I suggest that from time to time a major production in English (in possible collaboration with drama, art, dance, music and film) is based on a theme taken directly from the local community. It might be documentary in form but not necessarily so. It might be based on work-experience in the community, an exploration of social conflict, an evocation of community life 'then and now'. Whatever themes were chosen, the aim would be to faithfully represent the truths (not the conventional platitudes) of the community to the community so that they could be consciously recognized and understood.

Fifthly, I suggest – it is the major contention of this book – that the English department, as general practice, works collaboratively with the other expressive disciplines so that key resources can be shared and public occasions carefully planned. One expression of such a collaboration could be a yearly arts festival in which the school would be open for the production, presentation and evaluation of a whole variety of work, coming from both the school and the surrounding community.

Finally, I suggest that writers – novelists, poets, essayists, biographers, playwrights and performers – are frequently invited into the school to share their work and to discuss, quite practically, the technical and practical problems of writing and performing.

In this way the conditions necessary for the fulfilment of the last two phases of the art-making process could be built up by the English teacher. In the second chapter, describing the last phase of art-making I wrote:

The final stage of the art-making process lies with the audience, in their response to and evaluation of the art that has been produced. Do the forms embody the secrets of their own hearts? Does the art delight, disturb, reveal the enduring lineaments of the psyche? Does it tell the human truth, however darkly strange and demanding? Or is it sham? Ego writ large? Mere cosmopolitan flash? Or is it caught in the very platitudes from which individuals struggle to free themselves, looking at art for the wider meaning? Without a discriminating audience, the integrity demanded by the earlier art-making phases is liable to falter and fail.

There is no reason to believe such an audience simply exists. But it can be built up slowly by the traditions of a school. It may be all but impossible to realize. Yet the nearer a school can get to it, the more it can secure the proper ground for an aesthetic education. Art is not merely a private matter; it is the means of emotional growth for a civilization.

In this chapter I have sketched the practice of English within the arts. I have argued that the English teacher had to guide the creative act through the five phases of art-making; that he has to relate the creative act of the child to the great creative acts of the received culture; that he has to encourage a living experimentation with the forms in the culture and an appreciation of those forms in their own right; that he has, somehow to promote the highly personal stammerings for meaning (as the sleeping images move towards the light) while, at a different time, securing the objective conditions necessary for art-communication. His responsibility is to see that each phase of the art-making process is allowed for and that it is rooted, wherever possible, in the best of the received and living culture. I have tried to hint at the practice which would follow from these principles, a practice which may seem strange to many English teachers but one which is familiar to most arts teachers and one which, I have argued, truly fits the very meaning of our discipline.

4

Preparing Students to Teach English as Art

A SERIES OF LETTERS WITH AN INTRODUCTION AND A CONCLUSION

I

I have attempted to describe an emerging concept of English as an Arts-discipline rooted in the dynamics of the creative process and the received heritage. I want now, in the most immediate manner, through a series of letters, to explore the implications of my argument for the training of English teachers. I am myself responsible for organizing and running, with the indispensable help of teachers in the surrounding schools, the English part of the Postgraduate Certificate in Education course at the University of Sussex. In this chapter I want to give the reader a sense of this exacting course, particularly the University side of the work in English. I must admit that my intention is shot through with hesitancy, for I know I am still groping towards the right course; I am highly conscious that I have not yet been able to establish the full conditions necessary for the fulfillment of an ideal. Voices within me advise caution. Should I not wait until I have fully established what I am stumbling towards? At this stage, surely, it would be wiser to stay silent? Other voices tell me that these questions are defensive and even false. For the ideal always moves beyond our hold, and the notion of perfection inhibits our movements. The educational process is unending and elusive. It has to be accepted in all its incompleteness, all its vexing uncertainty.

At the best of times, it is a massive struggle to locate the right concepts for what one wants to do or, indeed, for what one is actually now doing. And, more often than not, the attempt remains incomplete, radically broken. So often the experience in the workshop or classroom defies conceptual-ization. . . . Inexorably, teaching moves beyond our grasp . . . and we are left alone, in the evening, sensing in ourselves a subterranean current of frustration. And even when the good moment in teaching has happened, we doubt it. Teaching makes us all neurotic, unless we can accept, in good faith, the principle of education as process, come to find a creative centre within ourselves, and learn to trust our fellow-colleagues and fellow-students.

These spontaneous reflections give me the courage to keep to my design. I must now describe to my reader the unusual method I will use in this chapter. Before a recent PGCE English course commenced I decided to try and capture the year's experience and to think about the pedagogic principles informing it by writing through the two main teaching terms a series of open letters to my English students. The practice would compel me to think about what I was doing – urging me to think, as I phrased it in the last chapter, *within existence and not outside it*. It also meant that, as I could theorise in the letters, I was able, more easily, to turn what I had previously run as academic seminars into practical workshops. In all there are four letters by me. But the students replied to my first three letters and a selection from their forthright responses forms appendix 2 of this book. I believe that the best way I can give my reader an indication of the style of training necessary for expressive English, is by reproducing, without any significant alteration, these letters. I hope they convey a vivid sense of *the experience* of teaching English as an expressive discipline.

However, it is necessary that I first briefly place the letters, and their various concerns, in the wider context of the PGCE course at the University of Sussex. The course has been described as the only existentialist course in the country, a course stressing the responsibility of the student to integrate on his own terms, through a personal journal (called 'the course file') all the diverse experiences – in the classroom, the school, in the university lecture workshop and seminar – which make up the year. It is also known as a school-based course for, during the first two terms, the teaching practice and the University work are kept in continuous dialectical play (the student spending the first three days of each week in the same school, the last two days back at the University). In the Course Document the distinctive features of the University's course are delineated as follows:

WHAT IS THE PHILOSOPHY BEHIND THE COURSE?

The Sussex PGCE course is distinctive in three important respects:
(a) the training is school-based: teachers in the schools are appointed by the University to take a major responsibility for supervising the student's training experience;
(b) three days of each week are spent by the students in the school, two days in the University – running concurrently throughout the school terms for the first two terms;
(c) the course is not assessed by formal examination or 'grades': assessment is on a pass/fail basis.

These features reflect the commitment of the University to the belief:
(a) that students learn the craft of teaching best by working alongside experienced colleagues and sharing the life of a school over an extended period
(b) that 'theory' should feed off 'practice'

(c) that the competitive grading of students on a professional course is both invalid and unnecessary.

The emphasis on the student working in the classroom alongside experienced teachers is particularly marked. In each school that I use for English a teacher becomes formally responsible not only for initiating the student into the practice of teaching, but also for advising the students and, at the end, evaluating his work. The Course Document insists:

> The teacher-tutors are pivotal figures in our scheme, the anchor person for each student.

As the open letters assume an understanding of the relationship between student and teacher-tutor and furthermore, as they tend to concentrate on the work I do, as curriculum tutor, at the University on a Thursday morning, it is necessary that the reader has an adequate understanding of the school dimension where the teacher-tutor has a crucial part to play. In a handout which I give English students in the first week of the course, the approach to school practice under the guidance of the teacher-tutor is outlined as follows:

> In the first term, as a rule, you will not be expected to tackle large classes but will be asked to work alongside experienced teachers of English in an active and collaborative manner. Obviously this partnership, with the teacher, initially, in the strong position, will take different forms, e.g. you might become responsible for the work of a small group within the class, might take off half the class to tackle drama or discussion or reading relating to the main theme, might open and direct certain lessons etc. Such an introduction will provide an established structure and authority and yet also a freedom to contribute and find your own way in. Within such a sympathetic framework, it is hoped that confidence, exchange of interpretations, collaboration on the syllabus, will quickly flourish. Such a pattern would, it is felt, provide a more subtle initiation into classroom realities *and* possibilities than the traditional one of being left with a class of unknown pupils with the joint burden of becoming responsible, at once, for the syllabus and the discipline.
>
> Throughout the first term particularly, you should seek every opportunity of watching teachers at work across the whole range of subjects, and perhaps become actively engaged, if only for a short period in the teaching of at least one other expressive discipline, drama/art/music/film.
>
> During the first term it is generally thought that the time should be roughly divided in the following manner: one third of the time on preparation, one third of the time teaching, one third of the time watching. In the second term, as a general guide, it is thought that the amount of teaching should be slowly increased.
>
> It is generally in the second and third terms, then, that you will be expected to become responsible for the teaching of full classes across the whole range, from the first year to the sixth form, (where possible). As English students are placed in pairs, we would like to think that, *at least*, with one class you would consider working together, team-teaching.

Various tensions, often unresolved, develop between the school and the University. The school insists pragmatically on what will work. The University tends to insist on ideal, theory, and purity of principle. At its best the tension established *is* creative: the philosopher is forced to face the compelling necessities of contemporary schools: the teacher is forced to think about the intrinsic meaning of his daily work. Thus, the tension fosters true thinking. But, at its worst, the 'sides' become polarized and the student stumbles, quite painfully, through dislocated worlds, a school to which he adapts on Monday, Tuesday and Wednesday, and a university where he resorts on Thursday and Friday to being like an undergraduate student again, arriving late for seminars, missing lectures (which are not compulsory) and letting the time hang slack. In the student replies (see appendix 3) some of the frustrations of the course are openly raised by my English students and I will raise them again at the end of the chapter.

I trust this quick sketch of the PGCE course's structure and intentions, provides the reader with a sufficient background to the four letters which, with the briefest preface, now follow. Those interested in further details of the course's general structure are asked to turn to appendix 1.

II

FIRST OPEN LETTER TO PGCE ENGLISH STUDENTS: THE ART OF WRITING IN PRACTICE

In the PGCE induction week at the University I met my group of English students for three sessions. In the second two sessions I moved immediately and without apology into creative work. This opening letter is a reflection on what happened in those two workshops and why it was so important.

We have, I feel, begun well. In spite of certain inevitable apprehensions, you have written two pieces of work, one with its origin in an object I presented you with, the other with its source inside your own experience. Furthermore, we have made a cassette recording of a number of the pieces. All this – in less than three and a half hours!

In fact, you were probably alarmed at the speed with which I moved. This was necessary. I was sure that only by dramatic action could the thick ice which separates individuals when they come together for the first time in a group, be melted. It is also frequently the case that the academic study of literature develops the most formidable inhibitions in students with regard to their own creative talents. As great literature rises on one side of the scale, so, on the other, descends the individual's own creativity. As we shall discover, this need never happen, should never happen, but, at the moment, it invariably does and is part of a broader pattern where intellect is developed at the expense of the emotional, imaginative and sensuous. Anyway, I felt that if such inhibitions existed among you, it was best not to intellectually discuss them, but rather to destroy them, to demonstrate, in brief, that you could write, in a very short period of time, both personally and effectively. There is no real problem here because it is the nature of human nature that it desires to express itself, to give shape to its experience so that it can simultaneously possess itself and transmit itself to others. All the arts derive from this basic desire to express:

> Each mortal thing does one thing and the same:
> Deals out that being indoors each one dwells;

Selves – goes itself; *myself* it speaks and spells;
Crying What I do is me: for that I came.[41]

(*Hopkins*)

The challenge is to undo false learning, to take off the shabby coat of bad habits we have been urged to put on. More positively, I felt that if I could find the right context and procedure and authority, I could release in you that innate desire to express and shape all that we know, feel and touch in the world. Later in this letter I want to analyse that procedure a little further. Here I wish merely to recall that I moved in with the imperative 'Write or else!' and even kept time – counts. And you all wrote, for the best part, with an honestly and accuracy which I could only respect and appreciate. The ice had been melted and the water beneath, unlocked, was rising and ready to flow.

I want now to reflect more generally on what will be our Thursday morning curriculum workshops. The word workshop – as opposed to seminar – is quite deliberate. I want our meetings to be largely devoted to the making of artefacts – of poems, stories, songs, fables, improvisations, plays. I want us to sense on our own pulses that the writer is a maker, a labourer, constructing in language enduring forms of felt consciousness. I want us to explore together the numerous possibilities for expression, to struggle with the art of writing and the art of presentation and the art of criticism and, inevitably, the art of teaching. I am anxious that we do not discuss creativity at a merely theoretical level but that we all, to a significant degree, experience it as an impeded but real movement from within outwards. I want you to know about creativity because you have experienced it and reflected for yourself upon its nature. The principles will emerge not from the pages of a textbook but slowly and tentatively from our practice of making (though, of course I cannot deny that certain principles are already present determining what it is we choose to do). However, the emphasis on the experiential – *I know because I have done* – is fundamental to any proper workshop. As the weeks pass we must become more and more open, stepping all the time from the little we know out into the vast unknown.

How does such work relate to teaching? I do not want to meet this question in detail here. I would rather meet it at the end of workshops when we can analyse together what we have done and consider its implications for teaching. In the first term I do not want you to worry over much about whether you can transfer the experience of the workshop to the classroom. I want you to give yourself to the work in hand without practical worries about pedagogy. *I want you to be selfish.* I want you to put to yourself the question 'Well what can I get out of this *for me*?' and not be ashamed. You see, this is not irresponsible. Before you can teach well, you must be a self-sustaining individual with your own alert life, quite independent of the classroom. I am convinced that creative teachers *are* creative because they have kept in touch with their own hidden sources of emotional energy. If one is to remain an alert teacher, one must not live only for the class otherwise the level of your consciousness will drop to that of the class and you will then become a companion rather than a guide. One must continue to be an intellectual adventurer, quick to pitch tent on the fluctuating boundaries of the known. One must continue to develop and refine one's own talents. And all this, as *a precondition for teaching*. As soon as teachers stop learning, they stop teaching. They begin to teach by rote and their subject disintegrates into a mass of dry husks as the terms pass by. Is it because teachers have, for many reasons (mostly to be sympathised with), presented their knowledged as the dismembered bits of a dead body, that there is so little respect for learning and making in our society? I suspect it is part of the answer.

In brief, see the workshops selfishly, see what you can draw from them that quickens your own life, your own delight in language, your own powers as a creative being. Paradoxically, in this very way, they form an indispensable training for teaching.

What qualities are important in such a workshop? I would like to italicize two fundamental and related qualities. The first quality is a readiness to give yourself to the activity of making, a willingness to throw yourself in, discarding the usual academic defences of cleverness, ironic reserve, intellectual judging and placing. The first quality is a readiness to risk yourself in order to find out something not yet known. The second quality makes the first one possible; it is trust. We must generate among ourselves an unconditional respect for the other, a respect which enables the other to give what he has made, knowing that the effort, and what it symbolises, is affirmed. Such acceptance does not preclude criticism. On the contrary it makes criticism valuable because once we have accepted each other at a profound level we are then ready to learn from each other. There is nothing more unloving than false praise. Criticism is also an art with a creative intention but only where there is a prior willingness to risk and a prior readiness to trust. Once again, it is a matter, perhaps, of shedding bad habits. How much of our education in schools has depended on competitive comparison, on graded marking, and, even more deadly, the assumption that there is only one right answer which the teacher and the textbook have infallible possession of? Here, once more, the problem is best conceived of as an unlearning of what has been all too painfully learnt. A *via negativa* but to a positive truth. Education can be both highly individual and highly collaborative: individuation and collaboration are not antithetical but, in fact, complementary. To achieve either, we need both.

The first aim of the workshop is *to make*. From this central experience I hope we will be able to:
(1) understand through our own experience the nature of creative activity
(2) hammer out forms and structures for the releasing and holding and refining of creative energy
(3) begin to define a concept of English as an expressive discipline and work out its relationship to the other arts
(4) consider ways in which emotion, sensation, intuition, memory, imagination, 'divergent thinking', can be actively developed
(5) move nearer to an understanding of the art of teaching.

And, no doubt, as we move forward, other aims, of major importance, will become visible. The doors of the house must be left, if not always fully open, at least, always ajar, to let in the urgent visitor with new aims; unexpected, but vitally relevant, perceptions and conceptions.

I would like now to reflect briefly on the first two workshops. You will remember how in the first workshop I arranged the tables in the manner of certain modern classrooms where children sit not mechanically lined up before the teacher but informally clustered round him in small groups. You will remember I distributed blank sheets of paper – and we had to wait, as is so often the case in schools, for late individuals to arrive. When we were all assembled I presented each of you with an encased horse-chestnut and asked you to feel it, to examine it and to let your mind play over it. I was, of course, quite deliberately working in the manner of an English teacher in a contemporary classroom and you were my pupils! I am sure you felt vulnerable and, perhaps, even a little resentful. For my part, I was relieved you did not play me up! I must tell you how nervous I felt. I had spent most of the previous night doubting the exercise. In my experience, thinking out a new approach can release intense anxieties and, at the same time, an almost overwhelming desire to revert back to tradition, to unambiguous and established ways of working. For the old patterns give security to both sides, the initiator and the initiated; and because they have become commonplace arouse no anxiety, no dread, no doubt. But simply because they do not arouse these negative emotions, they tend not to excite the more positive ones either. To teach creatively in my experience entails this conflict of simultaneously *wanting* and *not wanting* to put in practice the new idea. Somehow one must try not to suppress the conflict but struggle to transcend it. After all, even if an experiment fails, we have more to learn from it than if we have merely parroted the accepted formulae.

When you had all received your horse-chestnut, I said quickly: 'Right, I will give you three minutes to evoke in words the quality of the object.' I gave you precisely three minutes and then asked you to open the shell and contemplate what was inside, to sense the nature of the inner husk and the conker it had protected. I gave you three further minutes to make quick jottings. After that, I asked you to jot down any associations or memories that the object released in you. Finally, you will remember, I gave you ten minutes to make one coherent passage. 'Find a pattern running through the notes. Create from the raw material something that is unified. Something shaped.'

When the ten minutes were up, we relaxed (but briefly) and then I asked you to read out your work. The pieces had been written in twenty minutes, the first pieces that some of you had written for years, and yet I felt, as you read them, that they possessed honesty, imagination and accuracy. I was impressed, and moved.

I like the way one of you turned the horse chestnut into a metaphor for the general state of embarrassment:

> But they are standing self-consciously on the table and are a little bit weedy. I think they dislike being exposed.

The same metaphor was, I felt, present, though perhaps unconsciously, in the following:

> Well you may have spines but I can still pick you up, slice you open with my nails

and look – there's your secret, not yet hard but brown and shiny, nestled in your
sweet white womb. I knew from your exterior you had something to hide.

Was I doing to you what you were doing to the conker? I think the experience –
of me urging you out of your protective defences and you urging the conker out
of its – is being symbolised in both the above passages.

In other pieces I liked the loving accuracy of description. The marks of the
brown conker being described by one of you as:

ripples in a stagnant pool of iron

I find that image precise, original and arresting. Elsewhere the imagery of birth
was developed by one of you:

With a crunch the bulb is
    opened revealing the pure
        white womb inside
Exposing the fresh, brightly golden
        brown seed
New born
Softly polished oak pattern,
        premature white patches
Baby smooth to touch.

There the metaphor runs through each line – womb, seed, new born, premature,
baby smooth – with impressive consistency, only thrown out by 'softly polished oak pattern', which, in later revisions, would (I feel) probably have to
go.

I liked particularly the philosophical opening of the following:

Now, the conker is a paradoxical object. Its shell is a solid, green sphere whose
spikes are sharp yet pliable and whose inside is soft, smooth and white.

I was struck by the direct lecturing tone and felt it might gain by being written in
free verse, tightened up and taken further.

Of the pieces I saw, I felt the following three came closest to being finished –
though, I believe, they can all gain from further revision.

We stand below, hurling sticks at the branches
Running to gather our spoils.
Held in my fist, this one looks old.
Just a few protective, defensive spikes;
Others only half-formed,
Retiring, almost apologetic.
Opened – inside, out of the white
Altogether different, yet never a surprise –
Small, packed, strong and young.
A bright brown conker.
Is it big enough? Will it do?
Skewered and strung up,
Ready now for battle.
Can it challenge the old?'

———

Prickly, sea urchin like
The outer shell;
Green, brown and in places
Where scarcely touched
Velvet lined. Promising, but guarding

A wood rich treasure:
Autumnal chest of vital being.

————

It is a dried-up chestnut with
dried, but bent spikes and brown scabs
scratches in the green
where it was bruised by its neighbours.
Even the smell isn't very fresh,
The usual smell of a soapy apple.

It opened easily, exposed the veined white pith,
Damp with cococut milk,
The brown oily bead, whottled and knotted as a thumb,
The brown centre in the snowy, spikelashed eye,
The yolk of the chestnut egg.
The boys used to chuck stones at the chestnut trees,
Standing in their wide, green dresses, a rich
                              store in their aprons.
But it used to be better just finding them in the grass.

What, then, was I trying to do in the first workshop? After the session I wrote in my own notebook:

> The aim of the workshop was to encourage a personal awareness of the process of making. I was aiming to break the ice of reserve and the protection of academic discourse quickly. At the same time, by taking a simple object outside of the self I ensured that no-one took an experience which, at such an early stage, we might not have managed, or come to terms with. A creative effort was thus started but within an incredibly tight structure, in which time, content and procedure were all given.

You may remember, also, that towards the end of the workshop I tried to briefly indicate the different phases of the creative act. I suggested that they ran somewhat as follows:

PHASE ONE

The releasing of an impulse

PHASE TWO

Free jottings, recording various images, feelings, observations, associations in no logical order. This providing the raw material, as it were for

PHASE THREE

The conscious shaping of the raw materials in terms of an emerging pattern which, if successful, culminates in the final artefact (this may take minutes, hours, weeks or years).

With the artefact made there still follow, I think, two further phases.

PHASE FOUR

Presentation. How is the artefact best presented to the community? – etc. Through reading? Taping? Printing? Duplicating? Nor is the activity over here for the presentation demands response from the audience and this leads to the last stage:

PHASE FIVE

Evaluation and criticism

For obvious reasons, we have not yet entered the fifth phase of the work but we have in our first two workshops had immediate experience of the first four. I hope in a later letter to define more precisely the characteristics of these five stages. If the schemata is sound it must have important implications not only for the teaching of English but for the proper teaching of all the expressive disciplines. This is an important matter for later reflection.

I would like, finally, to draw this letter to a close by reflecting on our second workshop. In this session, I introduced Leslie Norris's 'Moondaisies' because I was anxious to indicate how the ordinary and the scientific can, at times, possess poetic power. I wanted you to know (something which, perhaps, you all knew. If so, bear with me!) that a poem could begin with the line:

They open from a hard involucre

and still be good. There is no set content or style for poetry. You will remember I said: '*To release true poetry we must destroy the poetic*'. I believe that there is no subject-matter which cannot be used in the making of poetry, in the making of art.

I read Ted Hughes' poem 'Wind' and R. S. Thomas's 'Welsh Landscape'. From there, with no discussion, because too much discussion diffuses the emotion necessary for writing, I asked you to select any landscape or object which, for you, was saturated with feeling. I think – am I right? – I gave you ten minutes for jottings (phase two) and about the same length of time for developing one coherent passage (phase three). You then divided into groups of two to prepare a series of readings from the workshops. Here we moved, more formally than in the first session, by recording our work on cassette, towards making a presentation (phase four). Once again, I found myself impressed by the range and quality of your work. Once again, your pieces had been written in no more than twenty minutes. Once again, the structures and strictures had released work interesting in its own right.

To some of you the 'exercises' may seem artificial. We have a notion, inherited from the Romantic Movement, of the solitary artist, waiting for inspiration to descend. But this view has become a cliché and like all clichés deceptive. Even Shelley, arch Romantic that he was, wrote: 'The source of poetry is native and involuntary but requires *severe labour* in its development'. Goethe proclaimed, 'The artist who is not also a *craftsman* is no good'. We need to develop a sober understanding of inspiration. We need to create contexts in which its offerings can be explored, developed, discussed and evaluated. To the solitary aspect of making we need to draw the collaborative; to the creative aspect we need to draw the critical; to the inspiration, the practical.

I have been reading with an unexpected enthusiasm Jerzy Grotowski's

Towards a Poor Theatre in which he is trying to analyse the quintessential quality of drama. In it he expresses the principle I am stumbling towards enunciating. Grotowski writes:

> the decisive principle remains the following: the more we become absorbed in what is hidden inside us, in the excess, in the exposure, in the self-penetration, the more rigid must be the external discipline – that is to say the form, the artificiality, the ideogram, the sign. Here lies the whole principle of expressiveness.[42]

Our task is to draw together the spontaneous and the formal. Like the fountain, the impression left is one of spontaneity but it is possible only through artifice. We have to labour to be spontaneous.

I have no choice but to speak in the first person. All that I say comes from only one perspective. Yet *the workshop, in fact, must comprise the sum-total of all our various perspectives.* I would, therefore, welcome your response to issues raised in this letter. Let us reflect together upon what we are doing, begin among ourselves the conversation of teaching and of learning and of making.

(October of the first term)

SECOND OPEN LETTER: THE PRE-CONCEPTUAL PLAY OF THE PSYCHE

The second open letter describes two more exacting workshops in which writing and criticism had been energetically developed. It concludes by considering, in detail, the second stage of the creative act, the stage when much of the raw material is given but where the shape is still uncertain and quite unrefined.

When I conceived the idea of writing a number of open letters during the term in order to clarify our work together I somewhat overlooked the inexorable pressure of events, the weighty load of commitments, which during term-time militates against such quiet reflection. Yet I want to keep to my intention because there is so much to be said about English and teaching English and so little time in which to say it. Nevertheless I do feel an obligation to prepare properly for all my other teaching commitments. So I find myself both somewhat divided in loyalties and without proper time to think coherently about the workshops. In fact, I am sure this expresses a key dilemma in education; a dilemma of which, I suspect, all of you have already become only too painfully aware. The existing realities seem to conspire against our creative intentions. In the expressive disciplines we talk a great deal about the development of individual consciousness for it would seem to define one of the legitimate goals of our teaching and yet we find ourselves working in conditions which often seem to encourage gregarious banalities and an underlying emotional and intellectual exhaustion. The pace of movement is too fast, the numbers too many, the content to be covered too extensive. The inner self, as a result, becomes neglected, tends to atrophy. It is the most difficult problem, a problem generated by a *personal concept of education* inside a system *of compulsory mass education.* On an average day a teacher must see between 100 and 200 pupils! How can she be concerned for the individual development of so many? And how, in such conditions, can she remain in touch with the living depths of her own personality? These questions are daunting but I do feel that they should *not* be suppressed. It is my belief that if we keep them in our minds long enough we may be able to find positive life-enhancing answers to them. At the very least, we will be in a strong position of keeping real, rather than pseudo, issues in the front of our minds.

In this letter I want to talk further about the art-process, that elusive and complex process in which good written work develops, and, particularly, I want to analyse the second phase of this process. If we can differentiate between the various phases of the making process we can evolve more and more adequate forms of pedagogy, more and more sensitive and coherent classroom approaches. Before looking at the art-process, however, I would like briefly to consider our last three workshops.

WORKSHOP THREE, 19 OCTOBER

This, you will remember, was the first workshop after your eight days period of induction into the particular schools of which you are now members. You found the experience so complex, so interesting, so demanding, so frustrating, that I felt compelled to discard the work I had prepared. So, we talked about English, English Departments and schools for three and a half hours!

WORKSHOP FOUR, 26 OCTOBER

As in previous workshops I arranged the tables in the manner of many classrooms. On the tables I had placed a number of objects: flints, foliage, toys, skulls, shells, etc. A number of you felt – perhaps all of you! – 'Oh God! No, not at nine thirty in the morning'. A few of you clearly felt the same panic you had experienced in our first workshop with the horse chestnut. Mary wrote in some notes taken before we started writing:

> Anxiety mounting, mounting as
> Peter talks my eyes keep
> straying to the objects on the
> table. Oh God what shall
> I write?

Perhaps that was a common feeling? And perhaps it gives immediate expression to a certain insecurity which would seem to be a particular mark of the expressive disciplines. I mean that in asking people to create poems or music or drama or dance we are often asking them to make something which does not yet exist and which has never been made before. The condition entails a certain anxiety because it requires that we move out, to some degree, beyond existing categories and the binding commonplaces of the everyday. It is for this reason that as creative teachers we must develop the art of living in a state of anxiety/uncertainty without being overcome by it. No easy matter.

Before asking you to select one of the objects for a starting point for your writing I read two prose-poems by the contemporary poet Charles Tomlinson. The first one was the following meditation on daisies:

THE DAISIES

All evening, daisies outside the window, have gone on flying,
stalk-anchored, towards the dark. Still, vibrant, swaying, they
have stood up through dryness into beating rain: stellar cut-
outs, arrested explosions; too papery thin to be 'flower-heads' –
flower-faces perhaps; upturned hands with innumerable fingers.
Unlike the field daisies, they do not shut with dark: they stretch
as eagerly towards it as they did to the sun, images of flight. And
your own image, held by the pane, diffuses your features among
those of the daisies, so that you flow with them until your hand,
lifted to close the window, becomes conscious of its own heavi-
ness. It is their stalks thrust them into flight as much as their
launching-out of winged fingers, all paper accents, *gráve* thrust-
ing on acute, acute on *gráve*. Cut the stalks and they fall, they
do not fly; let them lose their bond and they, too, would grow,
not lighter, but suddenly heavy with the double pull of their
flower flesh and of the rain clinging to them.[43]

The second prose-poem called 'Skullshapes' was, you will recall, a reflection
not only on skulls but on *the nature of perception*. I selected these prose-poems for
two reasons. First they struck me as interesting examples of contemplative
writing based on simple objects. Secondly, both passages struck me as being still
quite close to that early state of note-taking where the writer is quickly trying to
catch in words the nature of what he is looking at. If I write the second line of
'Daisies' like this you will see what I mean:

Still   –
vibrant   –
swaying   –
they have stood up through dryness
                into beating rain   –
stellar cut outs   –
arrested explosions   –
too papery thin to be flower-beds   –
flower faces perhaps   –
upturned hands   –
with innumerable fingers

There, one senses, I think, the alert mind of the poet struggling to define the
nature of the living flower as it sways before him. I want to say more about this
stage of writing later.

Having read two passages by Charles Tomlinson I left you to write for, I think,
about a period of thirty minutes.

After break I asked, quite remorselessly (I confess), for a second piece of work.
Here, though, the task was different. In the first piece I had asked you to build up
a piece of writing from considering the object in front of you. It was a meditation
emerging from an object 'out there'. In the second, I was asking you to
imaginatively identify with any energy in nature – wind, water, fire, frost, light,
darkness. I read, without much commentary, Ted Hughes' 'Hawk roosting' and
three primitive poems 'Praise-song of the wind', 'A spell to destroy life' and 'The
rain man's praise song of himself'. Again, you wrote for about thirty minutes.
Then we finished the workshop with a communal chanting of 'Praise song of the

wind'. I asked you to work on one or both pieces of writing and to let me have copies for duplication. In the very first workshops I had wanted to stress *presentation of work* (hence reading it out and recording it on cassette) now I was anxious that we should move towards criticism and evaluation.

WORKSHOP FIVE, 2 NOVEMBER

The whole of our three-hour workshop was given over to a collaborative and critical analysis of some of the work produced in workshop four. We set ourselves the following questions:

Can we locate and develop fitting criteria for the evaluation of writing?
Can we agree as to what the habit of good criticism looks like?
Can we couch our criticism in such a way that it is a positive rather than a negative force for the young writer?

For the most part we concentrated on the first two. I was reassured by the amount of agreement we found among ourselves with regard to the writing. There seemed to be a living and emerging consensus. We tended to agree, with inevitable exceptions and certain differences of emphasis, on what in the writing makes one piece vital, another dead. A widespread failing seemed to lie in a tendency to state rather than to evoke, to conceptualize rather than to imagine. This failing is quite understandable as our education has developed in all of us a ready desire to categorize, an ability to abstract and define (which is not to be belittled) at the expense of sensuous and metaphorical modes of exploration and expression. Quite simply, we have not been encouraged to explore the world through metaphor and image – and yet these are very deep ways in which the psyche makes living patterns of its daily experience, as, for example in its nocturnal dreams and daily fantasies. There are, I suspect, many experiences which can be presented and understood through image and symbol which cannot be grasped *in any other way* and yet we have not made these experiences or their immediate symbolic language central to our educational system. Indeed, quite the reverse. We have over-developed a conceptual knowledge which has removed us from the concrete actualities of our experience. Only too often we have been asked to convert the lovely and unique apple into the common abstraction of 'x'.

There is no need to rehearse our discussions. It is, though, worth pointing out it took us over three hours to discuss *six* short poems! *There is a great deal that can be said about any piece of writing and it would seem that there can be a fair measure of objectivity in such discussion.* It is only by guided discussion and illuminating commentary that most students'/childrens'/writers' written work can develop and mature. The creative enterprise depends upon such criticism—just as criticism, to be vital, depends on a creative purpose. Henry Canby has expressed the former principle and its implications cogently in his remark:

> Unless there is somewhere an intelligent critical attitude against which the writer can measure himself . . . one of the chief requirements for good literature is wanting . . . , the author degenerates.[44]

Criticism, on the other hand, cut off from a profound creative need, becomes, as it has become in so many educational institutions, mere academicism.

In our discussion on our own passages we were able to pinpoint at least two crucial elements in poetic expression. Imagery. And rhythm. This concurs, incidentally, with Ezra Pound's judgement in his volatile *ABC of reading*. Ezra Pound there argued:

> Language is a means of communication. To charge language with meaning to the utmost possible degree we have . . . the three chief means:
> I. throwing the object (fixed or moving) on to the visual imagination;
> II. inducing emotional correlations by the sound and rhythm of the speech;
> III. inducing both of the effects by stimulating the associations (intellectual or emotional) that have remained in the receiver's consciousness in relation to the actual words or word groups employed.[45]

Ezra Pound, employing Greek concepts, called these:

phanopoeia
melapoeia
logopoeia

and went on to declare shrewdly:

> Incompetence will show in the use of too many words.

Here, then, would seem to be some of the working elements for the effective discussion of poetic writing, though I am not suggesting that we should adopt Pound's Greek trinity of terms. I hope there will be further opportunity to develop the practice of living criticism in relationship to your own work and to the work some of you are now bringing in from the classroom.

I would like to conclude these reflections of our fifth workshop with a stanza from the contemporary Irish poet Seamus Heaney because I feel you may prefer his way of defining the elements of poetry to Ezra Pound's (though they are in substantial agreement as to what matters):

> Give us poems, humped and strong,
> Laced tight with thongs of song.
> Poems that explode in silence
> Without force, without violence.
> Whose music is strong and cheer and good
> Like a saw zooming in seasoned wood.
> You should attempt concrete compression,
> Half guessing, half expression.[46]

Finally, some brief reflections upon the making process in the arts. We have now had limited but real experience of the five phases of creative work which I listed in my first letter. I have begun by releasing (1) a generative impulse, (2) raw inchoate material. We have (3) refined it and shaped it into a single artefact. We have (4) presented it, read it out, recorded it on cassette, typed it up and duplicated it. And lastly (5) we have attempted to evaluate it, find appreciative/critical terms for our experience of the artefact.

I want now to return to the nature of the second phase of creative work.

In my first open letter I said that this phase was marked by free jottings, a recording of various images, feelings, observations, associations in no logical order out of which a significant pattern takes shape in relationship to an informing impulse. When you begin you generally do not know what the finished piece will look like. *The work grows through the process of writing*. Invariably one begins with inchoate intuitions, uncertain flashes of insight, certain rhythms, intriguing metaphors, vaguely felt conceptions, even stray words that seem to have a certain beauty or emotional charge. This first stage is, in many ways, the most problematic of all. Above all, we must be willing to make a mess, to let images, associations, suggestions, ideas, rise without judging them, without censoring them. We must not think about results. We must immerse ourselves in what is, dramatically or vaguely, quickly or slowly, easily or painfully, being given. We need a ripe passivity before our own mind, what Keats named 'negative capability', a willingness to be in a state of uncertainty without irritable reaching after fact or conclusion.

Another way of putting this is to say we must open ourselves to the unconscious. Here, quite obviously, we have most to learn from the practice of creative people and particularly the practice of committed writers. Arthur Koestler in *The Act of Creation* compares the poet to a skin diver with a breathing tube, who is capable of regressing to earlier more primitive levels in the mental hierarchy while other processes continue simultaneously on the rational level. The poet, while remaining in contact with consciousness decends into the unconscious: Koestler uses the word 'regression' but this is not, of course, to be taken as a negative judgement: it is necessary return to a more primitive level where symbolization tends to be highly visual, sensuous, metaphorical and indeed mythopoeic. It is now well known that many great creative acts, in the sciences as much as in the arts, developed out of imagery, unconsciously given. Friedrich Kekulé's key theory about the nature of molecules derived from dream-imagery (see pages 118 and 169–70 of *The Act of Creation*). Einstein celebrated a sort of pre-conceptual play of the mind as the necessary prelude to fertile scientific enquiry. He wrote:

> Taken from a psychological standpoint, *this combinatory play seems to be the essential feature in productive thought* – before there is any connection with logical construction in words or other kinds of signs which can be communicated to others.
> The above-mentioned elements are, in any case, of *visual* and some of *muscular type*. Conventional words or other signs have to be sought for laboriously only in a *secondary stage*, when the mentioned associated play is sufficiently established and can be reproduced at will. (my italics).[47]

The process one is encouraging as the prelude to the creation of imaginative work in English would seem to be the same sort of process which marks productive thought in all disciplines. It is also a 'thinking' which tries to go outside all conventional frames, all frozen symbolic forms, an attempt to return to the source from which all symbols come.

It is a matter of the conscious mind getting in touch with the unconscious. What we call inspiration might better be described as a swift invasion of the conscious mind by the unconscious. Goethe somewhere described the poet in the act of writing as moving with the assurance of a sleep-walker, knowing infallibly what to do without knowing consciously. But, at the same time, in inspired writing the speed can sometimes be so rapid that the writer can barely keep up.

C. M. Bowra in *Inspiration and poetry* has described this state well in relationship to the Russian writer, Pushkin:

> In many cases an idea may move faster than the words which pursue it, and the poet is hard put to keep abreast of it. We can see evidence for this in Pushkin's manuscripts. He will often write down complete lines and variant versions of them as if trying to catch the absolutely right effect, but no less often he will leave gaps and race after the next theme which lures him on, setting down a few odd words, a phrase or a rhyme or a mere clue to what he wishes to say. The whole thing seems to have been done at an extraordinary speed, as if the inspiring thoughts were often too fast for the words which pant after them. But so lively and powerful is the source of energy, so rich in suggestions and so actively at work in his consciousness, that he is able to come back to it and fill in the gaps later by reference to it. Though few poets work with Pushkin's speed and abundance, most know something like his condition. In this process, what begins by being almost unconscious becomes conscious; what is at the start an outburst of energy infused with a vague idea or an undifferentiated vision becomes concrete and definite; what is outside the poet's control is gradually made to submit to his will and judgement. Such, or something like it, seems to be the usual experience of poets, and such primarily inspiration is.[48]

In this process what begins by being almost unconscious becomes conscious. However, the conscious mediating mind must be there. If it breaks off, as Coleridge in writing 'Kubla Kahn' had his attention broken by the mundane visitor from Porlock, the emerging hulk of the poem can invariably sink back down, become lost forever.

The conditions in which 'Kubla Kahn' were written or partly written emphasise the nature of the conscious – unconscious interplay in imaginative writing. But, as I said in my first letter, I do not think we should become too romantic about the Muse. As writers and teachers we have to develop sober exercises, settled procedures for promoting a free traffic over the bridge between the conscious and unconscious. Most directors working in the theatre develop vigorous, practical and precise exercises to keep their actors alert and ready, exercises which simultaneously relax and concentrate the mind. The challenge is on us to create exercises which can release feeling and imagination and which can pierce the solid crust of ordinary consciousness. Henry Moore, to give one example of what I have in mind, keeps a notebook and in the evening allows major ideas for his sculpture to generate from a series of free doodlings and quick scrawlings. Opposite is a typical page from one of his notebooks.

Henry Moore writes:

> I still do drawings in notebooks usually in an evening as I sit by the fire after a day's work in the studio. But they are not drawings which I envisage being framed afterwards or exhibited, they are either sketchbook tryouts of possible ideas for sculpture or just scribbles in which one hopes that some new idea might come.[49]

From such modest and practical exercises has emerged some of the most powerful sculpture of all times. In the arts we must often become passive, in the sense of allowing and being open to, before we can become active, in the sense of selecting, shaping, making. We must fashion subtle means of drawing up the *prima materia* which only later we can refine and complete and present to others.

It is worth, here, drawing your attention to the philosopher R. G.

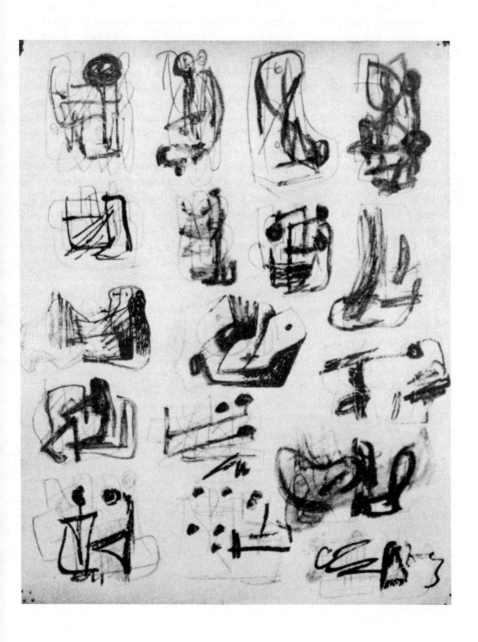

IDEAS FOR SCULPTURE, c. 1937. Henry Moore.

Collingwood, one of the few modern English philosophers to write at length on the arts. Collingwood distinguished between art and pseudo art by referring to the different type of process in which they are made. True art is always uncertain in its origin. You can never tell what the finished work will look like till the end of the making process. True art is, in its creation, a groping towards clarification. Pseudo art, in contrast, knows the end in the beginning. Pseudo art (meretricious novels, advertisements, Boots' reproduction paintings, muzak etc., etc.,) conforms to preconceived formulae. There is, hence, no discovery, only repetition, only a further reproduction of set skills and set materials. In other words, Collingwood is, at a philosophical level, confirming our notion of the messy inchoate beginnings of the art process.

What works against this habit of wise passivity? I would say, in my usual dogmatic manner, almost everything! We have been trained, as I said earlier, to think abstractly rather than to think concretely through image and metaphor, through touch and rhythm. We have been trained to judge quickly, and censoriously. We have been trained to divide the multitudinous universes of human experiences into such immediate and divisive categories as right/wrong, fail/pass, true/false, tick/cross. We have imbibed these categories so constantly in education that they fall upon the creative process, even before it can unfold, and judge it wanting. We condemn before we consider. We censor rather than create. We banish our own entangled mass of imagery and emerging insight because it refuses to conform to the narrower categories of our over-educated minds. The desire to classify, so powerful in us, inhibits the very sources of our own would-be-fertile minds. We must unlearn much of what we have learnt in order to learn again. In this new sequence we must needs move *from within outwards from the unconscious towards the conscious*. Because this is a sublime aim, we must be very practical about it all. We need forms, structures, exercises, methods: an A to Z of a new type of pedagogy.

I would like to conclude by reminding you of what was said at the end of the first open letter. Namely that these letters are, like most letters, there to be responded to and that, finally, the workshops to be real must include all our perspectives. Disagreement can often be more valuable than agreement. Opposition, as William Blake said, can form the condition for friendship or, in this case, the experience of education.

(November of the first term)

A Poem by Laura from the Fourth Workshop

A BIRD'S SKULL

The upper part remains,
Riddled, shell-white
Brittle as a leaf, feather-light,
The skeleton of a skull.

The small thinking cap
Behind the prying bill
That preened the soaking, flightless plumage of the sea.

This is a husk of light,
A soundless harp, plucked clean,
A holy relic,
A bone of contention between
water and wind.
No fire and brimstone,
Grimy dust on dust.
It makes a cleaner job of death
Than most of us.

THIRD OPEN LETTER: ESSENTIAL SKILLS AND TECHNIQUES IN ENGLISH AS AN ARTS DISCIPLINE

The third open letter was written towards the end of the first term. In it I try to draw the main threads of the term together. I am particularly anxious that the five stages of the creative process, now experienced, are understood and that their implications for daily teaching in the classroom made lucid. I conclude by wishing the English students a convivial Christmas, a break they more than needed and had more than earned.

It seems impossible but our first term together is coming to a close. How swiftly each workshop goes! And now as we move into December, I think guiltily of all that we have not done. Yet the process, the characteristic method of work, has, I hope, become clear. How, I wonder, are you finding it? What do you feel you have gained from your own writing? What have you drawn out for yourself from the collaborative sessions of making (in the case of the ballad and the frames, for example) and evaluation? What connections are you able to make between the workshop and the classrooms in which you are now busily teaching? It is still, perhaps, too early to answer with any certainty. The work we are doing requires great spans of uninterrupted time. The limited conditions and above all the constraints of time urge us to look for 'results' prematurely. We must – and I am in great part addressing myself here – resist this temptation, and continue to identify with the emerging points of growth, the underground shoots which hold within themselves the future.

In this letter I wish to draw together my reflections on the creative process and to indicate some of the implications for teaching. In doing this I will often only be making more explicit, the implicit assumptions behind our workshops. It should serve to clarify the process we have actually experienced. At least, I hope so.

You will remember that in the concluding section of my last letter I described the early stages of the creative process. I said that at this time the individual had to hold back the critical discriminations of his own mind in order to let the nature of the new reveal itself. The old has to be pressed back to allow space for the new. The creative impulse must be allowed to stammer towards its own truth. It is, invariably, a hesitant, awkward, absorbing, fragmentary, frustrating matter. It can seem, in very quick succession, fascinating, unbearable, pointless, and tremendously satisfying. At this stage of work the artist is not concerned with the final form: he is concerned to identify with the new imagery, rhythms, word-clusters, paradoxes, associations in order to sense their power and the direction of their thrust. It is a messy affair as Charles Lamb discovered when he saw the first draft of Milton's 'Lycidas':

> How it staggered me to see the fine things in their ore, interlined, corrected as if their words were mortal, alterable . . . as if inspiration were made up of parts, and these fluctuating, successive, indifferent! I will never go into the workshop of any great artist again.[50]

Unlike Lamb, we need not be surprised by the disorder of the creative process. We have inherited a more rich and complex sense of the psyche – after novelists like Dostoevsky and D. H. Lawrence, after philosophers like Nietzsche, after psychologists like Freud and Jung, we know how strange, enigmatic and perverse the psyche can be. We no longer expect 'truths' to be given outside of the endless and uncertain process of discovering them. Indeed *this very process* has become the major and most positive value of our times – which is why, for example, we prefer the unfinished works of Leonardo and Michelangelo to their completed 'masterpieces'. More practically, it is by entering the littered workshops of creative men and women that we can begin to comprehend the nature of the art-process and in so doing find appropriate ways for promoting creative activity in our English classes. As I said in my first letter, the discarding of the word 'seminar' and the adoption of the word 'workshop' was deliberate; it was meant to bear within it a whole philosophy of education: education as practice, as process, as the making of those cultural conditions necessary for individual and communal fulfilment.

I hope I have said enough about the first two phases of the creative activity. Ultimately, they are not to be analysed, at least not by the creative artist and perhaps not even by the teacher. They are to be recognised with some awe and to be allowed to enter on their own terms, to be given the conditions they require for their elusive workings. Marie Louise von Franz in her book *The Feminine in Fairy Tales* has said:

If you are artistically inspired and in the full surge of a new inspiration, you can be lamed by . . . interpretation and lose the thread. *The first welling up of a creative idea must never be disturbed. One should never talk about such ideas before they have taken definite shape* for they are as delicate as newborn babies.[51]

(my italics)

She is surely right.

But there is a stage after the impulse has been released (first phase) and the images and ideas well up into consciousness (second phase). You will remember in the first letter I called this '*the conscious shaping of the raw material*'. When, you might ask, does the second phase end and the third begin? In life all concepts blur. The two phases overlap, elements of the third phase will exist in the second, elements of the second still exist in the third. I think the change I'm anxious to register shows itself in *a change of attention* in the artist. In the second phase, he is anxious to get the material, in whatever sequence, in whatever form, in whatever language, down onto the blank sheets of paper. He is trying to keep his mind an open thoroughfare and is receptive to all that enters. Or, to change the image, he is like a medium sitting in a darkened room trying to catch the voices which are whispering or, even, shouting somewhere inside him. He has to be highly alert. Alarmingly open. In the third phase, the artist's attention changes. The mind now focusses down onto the accumulated material – it begins to organize in terms of an emerging pattern, it seeks to become an active agent in the cystallization of form. The writer is no longer a listener and a medium, but an editor and a worker. No longer passive, but strenuously active. And in shaping the *prima materia* he becomes aware, I suspect, of an audience, not an audience out there so much as an ideal audience sitting in the auditorium of his own mind. To this audience, as the second phase develops, he constantly throws an amazingly diverse number of questions, 'Do you understand this archaic word if I use it like this?' 'Has this image become hackneyed?' 'Do you get the double meaning?' 'Is it possible to use *this* word in a love poem without destroying its intention?' 'How do you spell . . .?' The questions indicate that the work is moving from the obscure personal sources of creative energy towards a public realm. In the public realm what has been made must stand not by reference to autobiography but to the powers dormant within the artefact (ar-factere) itself. The poem must live or die on its own merits. The artist is therefore passionately concerned to find the right form for his experience, representative form.

In describing the first two phases of creative work I celebrated process: *ultimately*, in education I would say, and have said many times, that the process is more important than the product. It is vital that children write personally so that they can grapple with finding shape for their own experience, so that they can find ways of possessing what they vaguely feel and vaguely know. We want them to sense the creative process.

And yet there must be tension *in the process* for it to remain alive. This tension is created largely by the need for form, for 'something to perfection brought'. *Form and process should not be seen as antithetical but as complementary terms.*

Like north requires south, like left requires right, like up requires down, so process requires form; and freedom, structure.

Without symbolic forms the process of experience would remain eternally amorphous. All human life is an endless encounter between experience and symbol, process and form. If the process of spontaneous living is to avoid banality then an inherited and living wealth of symbolic formulations is one of the necessary conditions. We are educated more through symbolic forms than, as Locke and the Empiricists thought, through the senses. If we declare ourselves on the side of process, it follows that we must also be committed to the ceaseless development of a whole range of symbolic forms which can be slowly or quickly absorbed into the bloodstream, to become our second nature.

I realize the above paragraph is congested with meanings and implications. However, I must let it stand. It is the best I can do at the moment:

> That was a way of putting it – not very satisfactory:
> Leaving one still with the intolerable wrestle
> With words and meanings.[52]

I am, as it were, anxious to defend 'culture' not as an end in itself, erected above life, but as a vital means, as indispensable means, to the realization of living. Culture matters because life matters.

The concern for symbolic forms (forms that are valuable because they have the energy to enhance, deepen and open our existence), has, also many implications for pedagogy. In the teaching of English it means, for example, that we must, with due sensitivity and tact, introduce as many appropriate forms for expression as we can find. It is no good to say to a class of children who have only ever written two page compositions 'Write it as you like'. Such an order will be interpreted as a different way of asking for a two page composition. We interpret what we don't know by what we know. I remember asking a second-year class in a Bristol comprehensive to write an animal poem. The class, before I had arrived, had seemed to do little more than comprehension exercises. Each line had to have a fact in it, and a correct fact, to receive the desired tick. The following 'poem' had been structured by the boy in terms of what his previous English teacher had always expected. Each line not a movement of action or feeling, but a fact!

THE FOX

The fox is a sly creature, it moves in a sly kind of way.
The common fox averages from 4ft in length and its tail is 14 ins long.
Foxes weigh from 15–22 lbs.
The females are known as vixen, males as dogs and little ones, cubs.
The fox hunts at night. The fox tracks down its prey by scent.
The fox likes to eat sheep and hens.
The arctic fox is white in winter and slatey blue throughout the year.
Foxes live in a place called a den.

(Third year boy)

For me 'The fox' is not very far removed from Bitzer's definition of horse in *Hard Times*:

> 'Bitzer', said Thomas Gradgrind, 'Your definition of a horse.'
>
> 'Quadruped. Graminivorous. Forty teeth, namely twenty-fourgrinders, four eye-teeth, and twelve incisive. Sheds coat in the spring; in marshy countries, sheds hoofs, too. Hoofs hard, but requiring to be shod with iron. Age known by marks in mouth.'
>
> 'Now girl number twenty,' said Mr. Gradgrind. 'You know what a horse is.'[53]

Both Bitzer in *Hard Times* and the author of 'The Fox' in real life had only been given one acceptable form in which to shape their experience, the pseudo-scientific, life seen as a bundle of facts. In such cases it would seem to me that the task of education is to open up *a whole variety of symbolic forms* through which experience can be explored and articulated: the imaginative, the scientific, the aesthetic, the deductive, the historical, the ethical and so forth. In the particular case of English – our concern – it means that the various forms for expressive writing are introduced and, where fitting, practically developed. There is a place in the classroom for the introduction of imaginative and expressive forms, as there is also, at points, for creative imitation.

Caldwell Cook, author of the influential *The Play Way* (1914), who was one of the first to grasp the importance of an imaginative approach to the teaching of English, and one of the first to put it into practice, wrote:

> First, then, consider the possibilities of imitation. A boy must read the masterpieces of literature, some very thoroughly and some very often. Then he may take some distinctive *styles* and deliberately set himself to write in imitation. But he must take them one at a time and, during the period of this practice, must scrupulously avoid mixing the characteristic elements of one style with those of another. Bible English is in a style which any boy can recognize whenever he hears it. He must, then, school himself to write in this style until his fellows on hearing him read his exercise can say, 'That is like nothing but the Bible'. Style is to be learnt, if at all, by example and experiment rather than by rule and prescription.[54]

I think Caldwell Cook was right in recognizing the value of creative emulation (mimesis) but was wrong in his approach. Instead of exercises in imitation, the challenge ought to be the one experienced by any artist seeking his own style. Namely: *to what extent can I convey my experience through this form*? To what extent can I shape my world in this style? Behind the experiment with forms lies an expressive intention not an exercise in cleverness. This experiment need not be, as I have said, always conscious. Often the influence of a particular style on a child or adult author is indirect, subtle and hardly noticed. We should work for a kind of creative emulation, not mechanical imitation. Absorb a style, then seek to transform it: this would seem to be the secret of artistic development, indeed of all cultural development. Goethe and Nietzsche both celebrated this law – the growth of the individual through the endless assimilation of other people's achievements, a cultural osmosis. Paradoxically, originality depends upon just such a receptivity. Henry Moore's work grows out of a devotion to the art of the 'primitives'. It is revolutionary, in some ways, and yet, equally, quite conservative, rooted in the archaic and powerful expressions of early man. It is the same with many other 'revolutionaries'. William Blake, the man born without a mask, was, as Kathleen Raine has shown, deeply aware of Christian and Platonic, Gnostic and Alchemical traditions, a man seeking to extend the meaning of symbols inherited from the past. Van Gogh, often invoked as the great original, learnt painfully from Rembrandt and imitated the work of Millet. Pure originality in the arts is, I would argue, impossible. 'As soon as we are born', wrote Goethe, 'the world begins to influence us, and this goes on till we die. And anyway, what can we in fact call our own, except the energy, the force, the will'. Nietzsche wrote that a person must be 'enormously multifarious and yet the reverse of chaos'. If we look at our own development as individuals we can, I suspect, trace the way in which we have absorbed other people's qualities and converted them into our own until they come to actually express *us*.

The introduction of forms, then, is an important part of our work. So is the introduction of techniques – particularly in the second phase of the creative process where the writer is concerned to shape and complete his work. Indeed, many of the words we use in the arts, in their etymological origins, italicize this technical side of creativity. The word poet derives from the Greek *poieen* to make – and, as you will remember, the Anglo-Saxons actually called the poet, *maker* (as, for example, in William Dunbar's *Lament for the Makaris*). It is the same with our word 'art': it derives from the Latin *ar* meaning 'to join', 'to fix', 'to put together'. Nothing 'arty' or 'high-faluting' there! The poet as a joiner. It is interesting also to consider that the Greeks had no generic concept for the arts but tended to use the word *techne* to extoll anything that was well constructed, skilfully wrought. Tradition would seem to establish a concern with skill and technique as being essential to the arts. It was, perhaps, the lack of this element which lead to the disdain for 'creative writing' in schools, which emerged in the early 70's and which is expressed, quite without judicious balance in parts of the Bullock Report. It yet remains true, I think, that writing can only thrive and mature in the context where skills and techniques are given recognition as essential elements in *the second and third phases* of the creative act.

I hope to have cast some light upon the first three phases of the art-process. I want now to briefly consider the last two phases.

I am sure that as English teachers we do not always give enough care to the presentation of new writing by our pupils. We generally see that the better pieces are read out well – and that is important. But much more can be done. The work can be typed up and duplicated. It can form the material for an anthology. It can be kept in folders of a selection or it written into the book which the teacher keeps recording the best work (according to the abilities of each child) of each class. The most obvious audience is the immediate one of the classroom (except in cases where the child has written for the teacher assuming privacy: I think this relationship of child to teacher which, at points, wishes to exclude the class must be respected. I remember many passages coming in from individual pupils with the request beneath '*Not to be read out*'. Here the collaborative workshop must be able to include within itself, the possibilities for more intimate relationships between child and teacher where the child can know that some, or indeed all, of his work will be protected by the teacher from the glare of public exposure).

Generally, though, within the impulse to make lurks the impulse to communicate and child writers, like adult writers, like to feel that there is a community of readers or listeners, however small, ready to respond to the new work. As I said, the first community is provided by the class itself but this, on certain occasions, should expand outwards to include the house (where a house system exists), the school, and the surrounding community itself. All good English departments produce fairly regularly a magazine for the dissemination of excellent work. In such ways the presentation of the work can be experienced by the child as a fitting climax to the imaginative act of creation. The existence of magazines, of poetry readings, of wall displays and classroom anthologies, in turn, encourages the life of the imagination and by being there affirms its value.

The last phase of the making process I described in my first letter as 'evaluation and criticism'. That strikes me, now, as a rather bleak way of putting it. Quite Gradgrindish! Allow me to revise it, please. May I call it first 'living response and appreciation'. Let us not be puritanical about the arts. They are there to delight us, to move our senses, to stir our imagination, to make our pulse move more quickly, to astound us with their power and depth. The arts exist to enhance existence, to confer a richness upon the lives of individuals. We must open ourselves to what they would say to us. We must not rush in with a defensive critical vocabulary. We must let them work on us, before we seek to work on them. Again, as in the first phase of the art process, confronting new works, we must be passive and accommodating and in no anxious mood to pass judgement. In this respect, I have been too hasty, I feel, in embarking on critical sessions in our own workshops. I should have allowed more work to be generated, and a more quietly contemplative attitude to develop. Majorie Hourd in her *Tract: On Creative Thinking* wrote:

> I have often noticed myself that when I have taken part in a literary study group, I have been prevented from any useful form of free association by the swiftness with which I have begun to judge, evaluate, censor and classify.[55]

Once again, for a time, we must hold back the classifying mind: right/wrong, tick/cross, good/bad. We must open enough to let the work make its mark on us.

Ultimately, we have to judge – but our judgement will be the better for our initial openness of response. How do we judge? Here I would repeat what has now been said so often since the time of I. A. Richards and F. R. Leavis. We can only judge by reference to the artefact itself. The poem is made up of the words on the page – and those words are part of a common language and a common culture. If a poem is alive it is because of the relationship of the words on the page and the power of these words to enact the experience of the writer. It is, therefore, possible to point to the words in the complexity of their relationships and indicate, in large measure, why they are so effective. Or, conversely, why they are so wanting. As we saw in our practical criticism session, premature though it was, common criteria for the evaluation of writing do emerge. In my second letter I described some of the crucial elements which make up poetry. Such criticism is important but it should, in my view, never be allowed to dominate the proceedings. It should exist to keep alert the creative impulse, as a means to refine and develop our own powers of expression and to increase our ability to respond imaginatively to the great art which already exists. Criticism is for art: not art for criticism. Thus it is that the last phase of the making-process (open appreciation moving to responsive criticism) can, thus, lead naturally back to the earlier stages. Seen as a whole and seen at its best, the art-making process has a spiralling motion. It constantly returns upon itself but at a different level. The movement is repeated again and again, but the altitude is always changing.

Having reached the end of this my third open letter, I put down my pen with a sense of relief. Now I look forward to reading your letters, delighted to put aside my intentions and wanting to step inside your actual experience of what must have been an exacting and, I know, exhausting term. And yet, to echo D.H. Lawrence, *look, we have come through*!

Have a good and convivial Christmas.

(December of the first term)

FOURTH OPEN LETTER: SHAKESPEARE, LITERATURE AND DE FACTO ENGLISH

The fourth open letter is an attempt to draw the threads of the course together. On 1 March we had had an evening seminar with teacher-tutors on Shakespeare in the Classroom. The speaker had such an alien and mechanical view of English that it served to sharpen the nature of our commitment to English as an expressive discipline. The letter begins by reflecting on this seminar and moves forward to consider approaches to literature, the expressive discipline of imaginative reading and the practical dilemmas of teaching English in the contemporary classroom. I do refer obliquely to other workshops and it may help the reader to know that in the second term the programme changed to alternating Thursday morning and Thursday evening sessions (with teacher-tutors). It included work on mass-culture, work on different concepts of English and, finally, work (with David Holbrook as visiting speaker) on the place of philosophy in English teaching and education. These sessions, lacking some of the intensity and continuity which, I feel, had characterised the activity of the previous term, yet opened up the complexity of the issues at stake and form the necessary background to this concluding open letter.

> Lorde God, howe many good and clene wittes of children be nowe a dayes perisshed by ignorant schole maisters.
>
> *Sir Thomas Elyot*

I am beginning this, my last open letter, on the 2 March. Last night, we had that frustrating seminar 'Shakespeare in the classroom'. The speaker, an external examiner and author of a number of widely used books in the classroom, had such a consistently sterile view of English that I know a number of you felt the evening had been wasted. In a sense, at the levels of both intellectual inspiration and practical guidance, it *was* a waste and yet it struck me, nevertheless, as a quite crucial meeting. Quite unexpectedly, it brought all our tacit assumptions about the nature of English teaching into an unexpected coherence. We all knew immediately, on the living pulse, that our understanding of education, English and Shakespeare was totally different from that held by the external examiner. It was impossible to delineate all the points of difference in the discussion which followed his talk – but the sense of a quite passionate disagreement was unmistakeable in the many questions which arose from all sides of the table. And, in his own defence, all the external examiner could do was to mutter something about *de facto English*.

What were the assumptions behind the external examiner's *de facto English* which angered us? I felt they rose to the surface not only in the actual text of the article he read but also in the examiner's casual asides thrown out between paragraphs. I didn't make a note of these at the time, but I recall to mind, for example, the following: the remark that Shakespeare was useful because he can always be quoted at weddings and funerals; the remark that if your headmaster insisted on a particular text and on certain examination results, you (the junior English teacher) compliantly drew from the external examiner's compendium of techniques the particular method which secured the 'O' level groceries; the remark that the 'natives overseas' simply love Shakespeare on their examination syllabus, although the external examiner couldn't see how the plays could make sense to them; and so on and so on. The external examiner's human position was, I believe, revealed in these asides while the actual article which he read *attempted* to embody a mindless neutrality, a listing of whatever had been done in the teaching of Shakespeare without regard to meaning or value. Facts without insight. Techniques without meaning. Practice without discrimination. *De facto English*.

Some of the external examiner's more poisonous assumptions could be listed as follows:
(1) that the English teacher should not ask fundamental questions about either education or English teaching
(2) that, as an extension of the above, the English teacher had to passively recognize the hierarchy of power as it exists in schools, and
(3) that, in the same manner, he had to accept the examination system as having the right to determine teaching methods, and
(4) that any approach (like *Coles Notes* and other mass-marketed drivel) which secured results was justified, and finally
(5) that knowledge *about* Shakespeare's plays was what mattered, a knowledge which, according to the external examiner, was now comparatively straightforward (unlike our knowledge about *Waiting for Godot* which, the external examiner suggested, still confounded the examiners).

Now these assumptions are so antithetical to those on which our course is based, that they served to dramatise the nature of our own commitment. We suddenly saw our world clarified with all its holding principles. In seeing what we are *not*, we could see *what it was* that gave our English work coherence. For as English teachers, have we not become committed to the understanding of education as process and exploration? Have we not come to see Shakespeare, like all fine literature, including that written by children, as imaginative experience embodied in words? Do we not see the English department as collaborative community rather than competitive hierarchy, and the school as a cultural and community centre, rather than an examination factory? Are these not the central informing principles behind our work, principles which may clash with what now exists in many schools (as they may also clash with *de facto* English), but which cannot, for those reasons, be merely discarded?

In listening to the external examiner, we knew, I suspect, that Shakespeare mattered for none of the reasons given. Shakespeare does not matter because he is 'Shakespeare', a colossal statue in the landscape of literature, but rather because of the particular vision of mankind that through the extraordinary richness of language, particularly through its metaphor and rhythm, and through the drama of encounter and action, is conveyed to the responsive reader/audience. In responding to this broad vision, with its endless see-saw of dark and light energies, our own humanity is enlarged and intensified. We see more. We feel more. We conceive more. We live more. And, surely, this is the case in varying degrees, with all good literature? And, again, as with all literature, we find our way into the work through an emotional response, through being deeply stirred by the power of words. Edmund Gosse refers to this basic experience in *Father and Son*, where he describes the effects of his father's readings from the Bible:

> The extraordinary beauty of the language – for instance, the matchless cadences and images of the first chapter – made a certain impression and were, I think, my earliest initiation into the magic of literature. *I was incapable of defining what I felt, but I certainly had a grip in the throat which was in its essence a purely aesthetic emotion.*[56]

In the classroom we want pupils to be moved in this way but, I think, we must also admit that there can be problems when it comes to Shakespeare. So what do we do?

In the first place it is, surely, the process we value, *the process* of children responding in a personal way to literature. *It does not have to be Shakespeare*. It may never be Shakespeare. Better no Shakespeare than Shakespeare done in such a manner that he is associated in the child's mind with infinite tedium for the rest of his life. There is so much good literature written for young adolescents today that I myself with a first, second, or third year would wish to begin with, say, such novels as Penelope Lively's *The House at Norham Gardens*, Henry Treece's *The Dream Time* and Ivan Southall's *Josh*.

The first purpose is not Shakespeare, but the initiation (where it has not begun) into the imaginative experience of reading literature. What is important is that, at the right stage, we can find the literature which engenders that immense satisfaction given by creative reading. And this, for many children in a society which gives scant respect to inner imaginative preoccupation, is a task exacting enough for the English teacher. When we have engendered the habits of sensitive reading, listening and interpreting, let us then ask, at perhaps the level of fourth and fifth year work (if then), whether Shakespeare *should* be tackled, and to what extent we can employ the more active methods (of improvising parts, of putting on a Shakespeare play, of comparing different taped recordings of speeches by pupil readers, etc.) mentioned by the external examiner. The question must always be: how can we help to give the imaginative experience the drama demands? But there is one approach which, for good reasons, we should avoid – the approach based on cut editions, on simplified versions, on, ultimately, the *Macbeth strip-comic* (which, of course, having been conceived in this mad century has now been commercially produced.) The reason for disdaining these educational 'advances' is that the power of Shakespeare does not lie in the extractable 'story-line', but in the totality of the poetic drama. To simplify the words is not to convert the experience into an easier symbolism, it is to distort and dilute the experience. Style and content are one and indivisible. 'Wash that filthy blood from your hands' from Macbeth strip cartoon ('All the thrills, terror and action of Shakespeare's great tragedy'!) *is not the same* as 'Go get some water and wash this filthy witness from your hand'. The difference in rhythm and imagery between the two lines constitutes a difference in experienced meaning. G. H. Bantock in the article 'Literature and the social sciences' from which I have taken this excerpt points out the metaphorical power of 'filthy witness' as against the literal 'translation', 'filthy blood'. Let us take on Shakespeare, if we decide as teachers to take him on, with all his subversive wealth, and not as debased coinage.

The external examiner's comment that it was a comparatively straight-forward task marking Shakespeare papers seems to me to indicate that we have made Shakespeare safe, 'a part of the heritage', an old mansion to be guided round on wet Sunday afternoons. We have seen this term how the consumer society turns culture into commodity, we now see how the examination system can do precisely the same to Shakespeare. Culture as commodity, from every side!

But it is not a new occurrence. I wonder how Shakespeare fared in your school studies? My 'A' level teacher stood before us dictating, for the length of whole lessons, notes from the back of his superior Arden edition and, when he was not giving us notes, he was, with a remarkable change of tactic, giving us paraphrases to do. *Knowledge about* had totally eclipsed *experience of*. Even now, I must confess, I associate these excrutiating lessons with the word 'Shakespeare' and it may explain why there remain a fair number of plays I have never read. My initial associations with the playwright are all negative.

George Sampson in his pioneering book *English for the English* (published in 1920) pointed to similarly inane and destructive approaches to Shakespeare:

> There is a well-founded tradition in a certain district of London that an old elementary headmaster, examining a class in *The Merchant of Venice*, and encountering the line ' Came you from Padua, from Bellario?' called for a map and insisted that boys should point out the position of Padua, and then the position of Bellario. The story is supposed to be funny, but it is really tragic. Its real point is not the comic ignorance of the headmaster, but the evidence it affords of the outrages committed in schools in the name of literature. No wonder children left school without regret, and shuddered ever after at the mention of poetry. It is still possible to use the present tense in that sentence.[57]

And, indeed, fifty years later the external examiner has, sadly, given us evidence for keeping up that present tense. *De facto English*, again and again. A dead tree which resists the axe and does not fall.

It is perhaps pertinent here to briefly draw your attention to the recent HMSO report on the primary school. The report testifies to a high degree of priority being given to the basic skills but little or no thought being given to the process of personal thinking and expressive making. Here again we find skills extrapolated from the active process of thinking, imagining and feeling, extrapolated and reified. Many teachers clearly think they have achieved what they are after with the slow inculcation of basic technique. They seldom seem to ask the fundamental question: why do the skills matter? Why are they important? And not asking the question, they fail to arrive at a true evaluation of the place of 'skills' in education, as vital but subsidiary agents in the imaginative, emotional and intellectual exploration of the child's evolving world.

On expressive writing, the report declares:

> The extent to which children were required to produce work set by teachers but not arising from other work or personal interests suggests that much less writing arose from pupils' own choice than is sometimes supposed.

> The writing of prose or poetry which was expressive of feeling, often labelled 'creative writing', was not as strongly encouraged as might have been supposed.[58]

On the development of personal thinking the report said:

> It was rare to find children presented with a writing task which involved presenting a coherent argument, exploring alternative possibilities or drawing conclusions and making judgements.

> But in only a small minority of classes at any age were children discussing the books they had read at other than a superficial level of comprehension.[59]

Furthermore the report commented on the deplorable practice of mindless copying:

> There was copied writing from reference books in about two-thirds of nine year old classes and in four out of five eleven year old classes. This was generally felt (by the Report) to be excessive. In four out of five classes children, on occasion, copied writing from the blackboard. The extent to which this was done was generally considered acceptable although it had too prominent a place in about a third of these classes.[60]

We find in the primary schools, a return to functional approaches; a loss of nerve and vision. It is as if Sybil Marshall had never written her brilliant *An Experiment in Education*; as if teachers were anxious to be seen as professionals imparting basic skills, rather than living initiators into the cultural and intellectual disciplines of the psyche-seeking-itself. One is left with the sad impression of many professional teachers earnestly working through work-cards and grading reading schemes, through grammar text books and information books, but without any comprehension of the true nature of education and without any recognition of the imaginative and creative energies (and needs) of the human psyche. It is not a question of 'techniques' versus 'creativity', but, as I see it, of technique *in relationship* to creativity. That, at least, is the notion which has informed the University-side of our PGCE work.

What comes out of the two terms' work we have spent together? Ultimately, it is a question which only you can answer. I know there has been considerable tension between idea and practice, between the philosophical formulation and the pressing actualities of the classroom. I fear this may be inevitable given our present schools and the present phase of our civilization. Furthermore, I suspect all good teaching has often to hold within itself considerable anxiety. We all cling to the status quo of our lives and yet education would have us move forward into something better: its nature would urge us to move out from the tepid shallows into the depths. Merely to accept what the adolescent brings is, surely, not enough? Surely we must also struggle to create those contexts in which he may become more than he now is. At the same time, not to accept what he brings to the classroom would be to destroy the middle ground – the ground between pupil and teacher – in which most teaching takes place. The teacher has to traverse an elusive fluctuating boundary between *what is* and *what might be*. This is never easy – but it is inherently problematic when there is not proper time for the relationship of trust to establish itself. Teaching, of the kind we have been invoking through the last two terms, is predicated on a tacit feeling of trust and this is often difficult to secure, particularly with third, fourth and fifth years. The relationship has to be tested, knocked about, destroyed and recreated before, finally, with some luck and some patience, it is accepted by the pupils. In my experience as a teacher I would say that there may well be some classes with whom this relationship is never properly established. It was certainly so in my case. There were classes that I disliked teaching because it was always a fight without any positive outcome and some classes can make you feel remarkably depressed, can make you feel like throwing it all in. And then, suddenly, one has a superb class with another form or there is a moment of recognition with the 'bad' class and one feels that, perhaps, yes, teaching is worth while after all, that, at high moments, the principles of creative education can inform and transform what goes on in the classroom. And so one keeps going.

I hope these letters have managed to make some philosophical sense of our experience together. I have been particularly anxious to explore a concept of English as a literary-expressive disciplines; I have wanted to give this concept a certain toughness of definition and a concrete pedagogy. I see the definitions and the pedagogy as complementary – both absolutely crucial. The definition would make English an arts discipline; a coherent way of expressing, exploring and refining experience, particularly emotional and imaginative experience. The implications of this for pedagogy are numerous and these letters have been primarily concerned with this issue. I have tried in these open letters to suggest the five-fold nature of the creative act and indicated some of its implications for teaching. I have tried to define the relationship of symbol to experience and its consequences for the teaching of poetry. I have tried to indicate the need for a shift of focus from the humanities to the neglected disciplines of art, music, film, dance and drama. I am sorry we have not had time to consider in detail the ways in which these disciplines might relate, collaborate and sustain each other. I hope in our last meeting we can spend some time on drama. In my view this conversation between the teachers of expressive disciplines is long overdue, and it is a conversation from which English teachers would have much to gain. The outcome of such a conversation could, I believe, have momentous consequences for the whole of the curriculum. Certainly the conversation would affirm the desperate need for an imaginative and inner dimension to the curriculum.

I would like to conclude these letters with a quotation from the Canadian critic Northrop Frye defending the place of literature in society and the power of the imagination in the psyche:

> Literature . . . gives us not only a means of understanding, but a power to fight. All around us is a society which demands that we adjust or come to terms with it, and what that society presents to us is a social mythology. Advertising propaganda, the speeches of politicians, popular books and magazines, the clichés of rumour, all have their own kinds of pastoral myths, quest myths, hero myths, sacrificial myths, and nothing will drive these shoddy constructs out of the mind except the genuine forms of the same thing. We all know how important the reason is in an irrational world, but the imagination, in a society of perverted imagination, is far more essential in making us understand that the phantasmagoria of current events is not real society, but only the transient appearance of real society. Real society, the total body of what humanity has done and can do, is revealed to us only by the arts and sciences; nothing but the imagination can apprehend that reality as a whole, and nothing but literature, in a culture as verbal as ours, can train the imagination to fight for the sanity and the dignity of mankind.[61]

There are many other issues I would like to have raised – both practical and theoretical. I hope these can be raised informally on Thursday, our last meeting. In this meeting I trust there will be sufficient time to share the individual experiences of the last two-terms in all their diversity, frustration, pleasure and complexity and time to explore further the nature of disagreements and necessary differences of emphasis between us. I look forward to that.

Finally, may I say how much I have enjoyed working with you this year. I have appreciated enormously your serious commitment to English and to teaching. I am particularly grateful for your patience and generous openness of mind. I would like to wish each one of you well in your various applications and every possible success in the new academic year.

(March of the second term)

III

The letters are personal and collaborative attempts to make tangible, within the terms of a PGCE course, the concept of English as a literary-expressive discipline. Ideally, I think a course designed to prepare students to teach English should ensure:

(1) that the student has ample experience of writing and presenting work in a number of forms – poetry, fiction, documentary, etc.

(2) that the student develops through discussion and production of his own work the habit of real but sympathetic criticism

(3) that the student has some experience of working in another art-form, e.g. dance, music, art, pottery, drama, film, television

(4) that the student continues to expand his own reading of literature and is introduced to modern and contemporary literature written for children and adolescents

(5) that throughout much of the course there is a continuous interplay between university or college workshop/seminar and classroom teaching practice

(6) that the student does some serious reading in the realm of aesthetics and symbolic philosophy

(7) that a personal journal is kept to order and integrate the demanding experience of the whole course.

The reader will be able to sense from the open letters that I am trying to incorporate these elements into a course which, in practice, is still far from complete. I suspect that many of the tensions described by the students (see appendix 2) derive not only from the three days in schools – two days in the University dialectic – but also from the lack of time to adequately work through the elements listed above. Towards the end of the course, students claimed that while the University work was 'constructive', 'stimulating' and 'important', the time 'was just too short'; they also felt that, in many cases, the discrepancy between the practice of English in the schools and the emerging concept of English as an expressive discipline was too great. 'The seeds', claimed one student, 'need time to germinate'. Certainly, much remains to be done and, perhaps, could only be done well in a carefully structured two year course of training. As I said in the hesitant opening remarks of this chapter, I am aware that the actual course I have outlined does not yet provide the full conditions necessary for the realization of all its aims. But it does represent a beginning, a personal attempt to put into action an alternative concept of English which it has been the purpose of this book to define and affirm. It is, I believe, a concept which many teachers, weary of the grey technicism of mind informing our partial curriculum, will, in the coming decades, turn towards and, through their teaching, develop, modify and extend.

I will conclude by attempting to clarify the place of English within a comprehensive curriculum and by suggesting a programme of change for the coming years.

5

A Programme for the Future

I

In this brief concluding chapter I want to put the case for English within the Arts in the broadest possible terms.

The philosopher R. S. Peters has described education as 'the initiation into public and differentiated modes of thought'. If we confined the curriculum to the epistemic communities of the sciences and the humanities, this might seem to be an adequate formulation, but it is simply not broad enough to define the meaning of the arts. For the expressive disciplines, while clearly differentiated, are preoccupied not with public modes of thought so much as *a highly personal mode of thinking through feeling, through the imagination and through the senses*, but particularly through feeling. If we decided to keep Peters' formulation we would have to radically enlarge it to include initiation into the personal and expressive modes of knowing. Perhaps the two definitions brought together, indicating a coherent initiation into feeling and thinking, into the forms of expressive symbolism as well as into the forms of discursive symbolism, provide the key elements for a comprehensive definition of the curriculum.

However, R. S. Peters' definition has another significance. His exclusive emphasis on the public and the cognitive is indicative of a civilization which confers little value to inward states of being, and which, for this reason, conceives the arts as luxuries, hobbies, leisure-time pursuits, methods of therapy, extra-curricula activities, entertainments and investments, but never as *fundamental ways of developing consciousness within a community and a continuous culture*. The failure of our technical civilization to comprehend the nature of art is reflected in every aspect of modern life, not least in our schools where, as we have seen, the Arts wilt in a state of disorientation and neglect. In the first chapter it was suggested that in our secondary schools only about five per cent of the time given to the curriculum is directly engaged with aesthetic experience, with art-making and art-performance. This is a national scandal and, until recently, it has been recognized as such by all the major reports on education from 1926 onwards. The Norwood Report in 1943 declared that 'the arts have not received the attention in schools which is due to them. These subjects are too often regarded as "special" when the one thing required is that they should be regarded as normal subjects'. The Crowther Report in 1959 maintained that 'most fifteen year olds . . . need to be introduced to the arts and given the opportunity to practice them. These are not the flowers but the roots of education'. The Newsom Report passionately defended the place of art, drama and dance in the education of those who had become disenchanted with schools or unable, for whatever reasons, to keep up with the more academic demands. But in spite of the recommendations and the good intentions, the expressive disciplines remain confined to the very edges of the existing curriculum and, in the sharp functional atmosphere of our times, are likely to become more so – unless there is a change of understanding among all teachers, and a collaborative attempt to create a comprehensive curriculum, faithfully reflecting the diverse intellectual and aesthetic forms of symbolic enquiry.

II

Traditionally three major symbolic forms of enquiry or what we have called in this book epistemic communities have been recognised: the mathematico-sciences, the humanities and the arts. I want now to briefly define the distinct nature of these three categories and to indicate where the subjects lie in relationship to them. Of course in any typology one must expect in certain examples considerable overlap and it is important to stress that while the categories remain independent they yet all interconnect and constantly influence each other in quite dramatic ways. The countries of knowledge may be 'divided and distinguished' but they are not self-contained. In the nature of things there is endless and busy commerce between them. Yet it is important that we recognize that each group of disciplines represents a unique integration of experience which has intrinsic value and has no need to go to any other discipline for its justification. Chemistry cannot explain history, science cannot explain art. Mathematics cannot explain mythology. This does not mean that we cannot find connections between the communities of knowledge, for, after all, these symbolic forms are creations of the same human psyche (they all come together in the consciousness of man). But, it does mean the symbolic forms possess an autonomy which, if intellectual life is not to become reductive and minimal, must be generously recognized. A comprehensive curriculum must equally embody all three epistemic communities.

The traditional differentiation of intellectual and creative enquiry into three major categories: the sciences, arts and humanities: is based partly on subject matter and partly on methods of procedure. I will now take each category in turn in an attempt to briefly distinguish their central features.

ARTS OR THE EXPRESSIVE DISCIPLINES

The characteristic concern of the expressive disciplines is subjectivity and its development through the making of creative forms. They are not concerned, in the first place, with 'knowledge about' but with the embodiment, through a specific medium, of individual experience, whether imagined or actual, or partly actual and partly imagined. Experience, in being embodied in sound, word, shape, colour, gesture, rhythm, is thus further developed and more fully felt and understood, first by the maker, secondly by his audience. The expressive disciplines are there to make visible the invisible, to give form to the inner world, to sustain and refine 'the intelligence of feeling'. The expressive disciplines are closer than the humanities or the sciences to the actual state of immediate consciousness; they unfold out of the rhythm of the body's movements, the pulse of blood, the system of breathing, the motion of the limbs; they unfold out of the spontaneous imagery and phantasmagoria of the unconscious and semi-conscious mind; they unfold out of the immense sensuous pleasures of touching, tasting, seeing, hearing, smelling; they unfold out of the innate desire to symbolize – and so share within the culture – immediate and otherwise ephemeral experience. The expressive disciplines exist to bring together, at the highest possible level, the individual and his culture. Their concern is the mediation of experience through expressive form, both the making of expressive form and the sympathetic study of it in the culture. That is at once the nature of the arts and their justification.

THE HUMANITIES

The humanities, being primarily concerned with the understanding of culture, are committed to the systematic elucidation of 'man-in-society' as he has developed in the past (history), as he exists now (social studies), as he has been affected by resources, landscape and general physical conditions (geography) and as he has given birth to religious beliefs and moral codes (comparative religion). The humanities focus their common beam on the social, on the complex relationships between man and man, between class and class, between nation and nation. They labour to develop a coherent understanding of man's condition.

The methods employed by the humanities are often broadly scientific in nature, resting on: the sifting of evidence, interpretation of data, certain forms of quantification and generalization, and the precise defining of concepts. They also require, at many points, imagination, intuition, sensibility. It would seem axiomatic that because of the complexity of their subject matter and because of man's own subjectivity *the human 'sciences', in their true scope, can never possess the accuracy or certainty of the experimental sciences*. The humanities culminate in the great problem of values, of ethical and cultural issues and dilemmas: issues and dilemmas which cannot be, in most cases, simply 'answered'.

In the humanities, man returns to man (for the object of study is also the subject) holding up a question mark, an enigma which demands elucidation but would seem always to defy total explanation. Yet what is lost in objectivity is gained in richness. What is lost in certainty opens up existential possibilities and the general critical play of mind over experience. Unlike the sciences, the humanities are primarily concerned with the meaning of man through the detailed study of all his human manifestations as they are recorded in historic cultures and in contemporary life. Their legitimate subject-matter, therefore, includes an evaluation of what is made in the arts and what is discovered invented/conceptualised through the sciences. Their unifying concern is the interpretation of man as man.

THE MATHEMATICO-SCIENCES

The mathematico-sciences work to conceptually comprehend nature; their key method remains the verification principle. A hypothesis is formulated and subsequently tested by a series of experiments. The hypothesis is then revised (where necessary) in the light of the experiments and, then, checked again. A truth in science refers to an hypothesis or model which continues to retain explanatory value. At least theoretically, such an hypothesis or model is open to and depends upon a collective verification, a common consensus.

The sciences, particularly physics, also use a deductive method. Here, the explanatory theory or possible model is partly deduced by logical calculation. It must be remembered that the ruling assumption of Galileo (and before him of Plato, although within a different system) *that nature was written in the language of mathematics* has been extraordinarily productive in our understanding of the physical constituents of the universe. However, in its pure form, mathematics is best conceived as an autonomous world, 'divided' and 'distinguished'.

As such, mathematics has no content other than the sum total of all the logical relationships between all its conceivable parts. If this is true – and many mathematicians would confirm the proposition – it means that mathematics is a pure symbolic form and stands, therefore, both inside science (where it is indispensable) and also, self-sufficiently, outside it. In its purest form mathematics desires only to draw out its own unfolding patterns into infinity. Thus under the category of mathematico-science I have, up to a point, brought together two related and yet quite distinct symbolic forms.

The following table is an attempt to represent a comprehensive curriculum based on my argument so far (see page 122).

A glance at the diagram suggests how the comprehensive curriculum, comprising the three main epistemic communities, engages and develops a number of opposing but complementary human qualities. The arts promote subjectivity, uncoiling from within outwards, from the self into the world, through the created artefact. The humanities are a fascinating compound of subjective and objective: when they become too objective they narrow their focus too much; when they become too subjective, they become expressive and enter a different dimension. The experimental sciences strive through the use of empirical methods to be impersonally descriptive. They come closest to objectivity but an objectivity which can only apply, at best, to the order of necessity, and not to all the possible meanings of the curriculum. The way we know quantum mechanics is totally different from the way we know the meaning of a work of art. In their respective dimensions, both acts of knowledge are equally valid. And subjectivity is as 'real' as objectivity.

If the curriculum is seen as a continuum which as one moves across it subtly changes its nature, the following complementary opposites can be discerned:

EDUCATION, EPISTEMIC COMMUNITIES AND THE CURRICULUM

Ends of education

The articulation and development of self
The articulation and development of understanding

Process

(Seen as primary, before differentiation of experience into symbolic forms) — From unconscious to conscious, from the undifferentiated to the differentiated, from the vague to the formal

Epistemic communities

Arts	Humanities	Sciences	
EXPRESSIVE (examples)	EVALUATIVE (examples)	MATHEMATICO – SCIENTIFIC (examples) inductive/deductive	
Art	History	Biology Mathematics	
Drama	Social studies	Chemistry Logic	
Dance	Human Geography	Physics	
Music	Comparative religion		
English	Psychology		

Characteristic concern

Expressive embodiment of experience within the culture	Understanding and evaluation of self and social process	Understanding of Nature	Understanding of Logical Relationships

Note: I have not included languages in the diagram. It is difficult to classify languages. Once they are half-mastered they come clearly under the humanities for they give access to another culture, a whole variety of new human and moral perspectives. It is the view of the author that much time is wasted on languages in our schools and that they should become available in the curriculum as important options in the fourth year and then taught very intensively indeed, in the manner of crash courses.

subjectivity	——	objectivity
existential truth	——	impersonal explanation
embodied feeling	——	detached intellect

The concerns on the left lead to the language of expressive symbolism thriving on multiple meanings, ambiguities, puns, associations, underground energies, emotional charge and felt complexity; the concerns on the right of the curriculum culminate in the language of discursive symbolism, of precise signs, working in a linear sequence, having one distinct meaning collectively established. As a result of these crucial differences, the sciences develop cumulatively, each generation extending the received methodology and tested knowledge; the arts, on the other hand, possess no such progress. They may have high and low periods but there is no way in which the cave paintings, the Gothic cathedrals, Michelangelo, Rembrandt, Henry Moore, can be surpassed, extended, outdated or falsified. Between these starkly described polarities, the humanities, being both objective and subjective, would seem to occupy a middle ground.

In stressing that the impersonality of science is one of its distinguishing marks, it must not be assumed that I am denying the existence of feeling or imagination in scientific activity. As was argued in the last chapter, in the preliminary stages of investigation these are essential qualities – *but these qualities do not make the activity scientific.* In the end, the idiosyncratic experience of the scientist is discarded to leave propositions which are completely abstract, devoid of all subjectivity. Louis Arnaud Reid has neatly indicated the relationship between feeling and science by pointing out that in the sciences 'feeling is an auxiliary' element whereas in the expressive disciplines feeling is 'intrinsic and crucial to the whole endeavour'. One *can* practice good science without any specific feeling. In the arts this is all but impossible for here emotion, feeling, instinct – what we called 'impulse' in chapter 2 – lies at the heart of the endeavour.

III

Our problem is that the arts as an epistemic community have been badly neglected. The problem is further compounded by the fact that English, for historical rather than philosophical reasons, has generally been defined as one of the humanities. One of the reasons for the confusion has been the constant confounding of English as a discipline within the curriculum with English as the medium of most educational communication. As I have made clear in the opening chapter, from George Sampson's *English for the English* (1920) to the Bullock Report (1976), there has been a significant tradition which has made it plain that *all* teachers should be concerned with developing the use of language as it relates to their discipline. What has been slow in developing is the realization that this illuminating principle releases English as a discipline to define its own intrinsic nature. It has been the intention of this book to argue that its characteristic concerns are literary and expressive – the development of identity through the creation and appreciation of the poetic word. Such a redefinition of

English lifts English out of the humanities and places it firmly within the arts. The precise relationship of English with the other arts awaits formulation. It may not be easy to achieve for it works against the established and entrenched practices of our schools. Yet it seems intellectually and educationally convincing, not only because it would seem to fit the nature of English as a discipline but also because it could be the great means for securing, for the first time in this country, a comprehensive curriculum where through the diverse symbolic forms of enquiry, all sides of the personality are cultivated and a sense of wholeness imparted.

What, then, can be done at a practical level to release the energy for a new configuration of English within the expressive disciplines? I would like to conclude by making a number of proposals:

(1) That the main work of the English department is seen as being literary and expressive in nature and that it should now ally itself with the departments of drama, art, music, film and dance. This could take many forms and in some schools might evolve into the establishment of a single expressive disciplines faculty.

(2) That, while each expressive discipline has its autonomy, forms of collaborative teaching between all the arts are encouraged.

(3) That the timetable should be blocked in such a manner that the expressive disciplines are placed together across any one year, thus making the collaboration mentioned above practically possible. The blocks of time should be generous, allowing for those spans of time – in some cases a whole morning or afternoon – in which creative work can not only be begun but be completed and, where fitting, formally presented. (But, of course, even in conditions less ideal, arts teachers can examine their timetables and find times for joint teaching).

(4) That subtle forms of evaluation of the expressive element in the arts are developed, allowing for work done over a period of terms rather than in two or three hours of anxious time. Here the portfolio of expressive work should be regarded as the norm, not the isolated analytical essay. (In the appendix I give the details of a new pioneering 'A' level literature examination).

(5) That for about a week in each school year (or two days in each school term) there is an Arts Festival for the formal presentation of the most vital and challenging work produced and that, as general practice, the poetry and fiction, the plays and films, the painting and fabrics, the pottery and the publications, the music and the sculpture are made a living and inescapable part of the school environment.

(6) That through all the classroom practice in English and the arts, a cogent philosophy of the expressive disciplines is built up, giving the work a strong conceptual foundation as well as structured teaching methods. Such a foundation and such methods are still, due to the prolonged neglect of the arts in school, badly lacking.

(7) That more in-service courses concerned with both the philosophy and the practice of the expressive disciplines are generated. Teachers of English and the arts need to explore and map the common territory of their work to discuss together the ways in which they might collaborate. Teachers also need to keep vibrant their own experience of making and need to experiment with the media and forms of different disciplines.

(8) That full-blooded courses in the expressive disciplines are offered in all the major training courses for teachers, in our colleges of education, in our polytechnics and in our universities.

(9) That at least some of the university courses in literature recast their teaching and organization in terms of an arts approach joining the practice of expressive writing to the study of it.

(10) That in our primary schools where the differentiation of disciplines is necessarily less sharp the whole environment of learning should be envisaged as aesthetic in nature, emphasising the drama of knowing (*theory* and *theatre* have the same etymological root), the discovery of pattern, the delight in making.

As English teachers our movements, perhaps, are best seen as being two-fold. Firstly, we must set about the proper practical and conceptual redefinition of our subject as a literary-expressive discipline. Secondly, we must work to make sustained relationships with the other expressive disciplines, ready to learn all that we can, yet informed by a sense of purpose, of a common collaborative community in the making. These two movements are not meant to describe two separate stages of development. Both need to happen simultaneously for each will extend and amplify the other.

The ten propositions taken together, and taken in the whole context of this book, call for the radical transformation of education. For the arts have a momentous part to play in the curriculum, which has still to be recognized (even, in many cases, by arts teachers themselves), and this part will only be fully comprehended when good aesthetic practice and sound thinking have been brought boldly together and at the same time the need for a comprehensive curriculum recognized by all those teaching within the partial curriculum of our modern schools.

It is time now for English teachers to redefine their discipline as art and in so doing help to secure a proper aesthetic education for our young.

REFERENCES

Introduction

1. Read, H. *The forms of things unknown*. Faber and Faber, 1960.

Chapter 1

2. Holmes, E. *What is and what might be*. Constable, 1911
3. Read, H. *Educational through art*. Faber and Faber, 1943
4. Sampson, G. *English for the English*. Cambridge University Press, 1975
5. Leavis, F. R. *The living principle*. Chatto and Windus, 1975.
6. Daiches, D. Review of William Walsh's *F. R. Leavis* in *Times Higher Education Supplement*, 19 September, 1980
7. Halliday, M. *The linguistic sciences and language teaching*. Longman, 1964
8. Martin, N. *Writing and learning across the curriculum*. Ward Lock Educational, 1976
9. The Bullock Report, *A Language for Life*. HMSO, 1975
10. Courtnadge, S. *A conceptual and autobiographical enquiry into the present state of English teaching*. M. A. Dissertation for the University of Sussex, 1980
11. Britton, J. *Writing and learning across the curriculum*. Ward Lock Educational, 1976
12. Sampson, G. op. cit.
13. Shayer, D. *The teaching of English in schools, 1900–1970*. Routledge and Kegan Paul, 1972
14. Quoted in David Shayer, ibid.
15. The Bullock Report, op. cit.
16. The Bullock Report, op. cit.
17. Oxford Local Examinations 'O' level, English Language Paper I, Autumn 1976
18. Advertising blurb for *English essay exercises for GCE and CSE*. Hodder and Stoughton
19. The Bullock Report. op. cit.

Chapter 2

20. Witkin, R. *The intelligence of feeling*. Heinemann Educational Books, 1974
21. Witkin, R. Ibid.
22. King, C. PGCE course file for the University of Sussex academic year 1979–80
23. Muir, E. *An autobiography*. Hogarth Press, 1954
24. Jung, C. *Memories, Dreams, Reflections*. Fontana, 1967
25. Mill, J. S. in letters to Carlyle dated July 1832 and July 1833 reproduced in *Mill's essays on literature and society* edited by Schneewind. Collier Books, 1965
26. Collingwood, R. G. *The principles of art*. Oxford University Press, 1958
27. Eliot, T. S. *Four quartets*. Faber and Faber, 1944
28. Dryden, quoted in Lancelot Law Whyte *The unconscious before Freud*. Tavistock Publications, 1962
29. Yeats, W. B. 'Long-legged fly' from *Collected poems*. Macmillan, 1933
30. Caro, A. Quoted in *The Guardian*

Chapter 3

31. Connor, A. 'Hill Top and Guy Fawkes' from *Lodgers*. Oxford University Press, 1965
32. Connor, A. account given in Robin Skelton's *The Poet's Calling*, Heinemann Educational Books, 1975
33. Josipovici, G. in the *English Magazine*. Vol 4. Summer, 1980
34. Collingwood, R. G. op. cit.
35. Thomas, D. quoted in *Poetry diversion 2*, edited by Danny Abse. Robson Books, 1974
36. Shayer, D. op. cit.
37. Powell, N. 'Making Poems', *Use of English*. Spring, 1979

38. Heaney, S. 'The Grauballe Man' From *North*. Faber and Faber, 1975
39. Diagram from *Writing and learning across the curriculum*. Ibid.
40. R. G. Collingwood, op. cit.

Chapter 4

41. From Gerard Manley Hopkins's untitled sonnet beginning 'As kingfishers catch fire'
42. Grotowski, J. *Towards a poor theatre*. Eyre Methuen, 1976
43. Tomlinson, C. 'Daisies' in *The way of a world*. Oxford University Press, 1969
44. Canby, H. quoted in *The black rainbow*. Heinemann Educational Books, 1975
45. Pound, E. *ABC of Reading*. Faber and Faber, 1961
46. Heaney, S. *Lines to myself* from *Death of a naturalist*. Faber and Faber, 1966
47. Einstein quoted in Arthur Koestler's *The act of creation*. Picador, 1975
48. Bowra, C. M. *Inspiration and Poetry*. Macmillan, 1955
49. Moore, H. quoted in *Henry Moore on Sculpture* edited by Philip James, Macdonald, 1966
50. Lamb, C. quoted in Phyllis Bartlett's *Poems in process*. Oxford University Press, 1951
51. Von Franz, M.-L. *The feminine in fairy tales*. Spring Publications
52. Eliot, T. S. *Four quartets*. Faber and Faber
53. Dickens, C. *Hard times*.
54. Cook, C. *The play way*. Curtis Brown Ltd
55. Hourd, M. *Tract 13: On creative thinking*. Gryphon Press, Autumn 1974
56. Gosse, E. *Father and son*. Penguin, 1970
57. Sampson, G. op. cit.
58. *Primary education in England, a survey by HM Inspectors of Schools*. HMSO, 1978
59. ibid.
60. ibid.
61. Frye, N. *The stubborn structure*. Methuen, 1970

Notes on the PGCE Course at the University of Sussex

The following excerpts from the University of Sussex Postgraduate Certificate in Education *Course document* give a description of the general nature of the course and a closer account of the place of the curriculum tutor and the teacher-tutor within the course. It is important to point out that certain elements in the scheme e.g. the place of the personal tutor and the general school tutor which are described in the full document, have not been included. The *Course document* is available on request from the Education Office, Education Development Building, University of Sussex, Falmer, Brighton, Sussex.

(1) WHAT IS THE PHILOSOPHY BEHIND THE COURSE?

The Sussex PGCE course is distinctive in three important respects:
(a) The training is school-based: teachers in the schools are appointed as tutors by the University to take a major responsibility for supervising and assessing student's training experience.
(b) For much of the year three days of each week are spent by the students in the school, two days in the University. In addition, the secondary students undertake a three-week block practice at the end of the spring term. For the primary/middle students this practice takes place at the beginning of the summer term.
(c) The course is not assessed by formal examination or 'grades': assessment is on a pass/fail basis.
These features reflect the commitment of the University to the belief:
(a) that students learn the craft of teaching best by working alongside experienced colleagues and sharing the life of a school over an extended period
(b) that 'theory' should feed off 'practice'
(c) that the competitive grading of students on a professional course is both invalid and unnecessary.

(2) WHAT CONSTRAINTS DOES THIS PHILOSOPHY IMPOSE?

The philosophy does impose constraints. The amount of time spent in the schools, and the sharing of tutorial responsibilities between school-based and university tutors, means that the theory programme at the University is necessarily thin, compared with many other PGCE courses. There are important areas of educational theory which are not developed on this course or are given less rigorous attention than they would be in other courses: for instance, the history of education; the philosophy of education; health education; comparative education. Other aspects of theory – the chosen academic discipline, the development of young children and/or adolescents, and the relationship of the school to the community – are studied with tutors who are specialists in the appropriate field, and often teach in them at all levels from undergraduate study to research supervision. The omission of the first group of studies is deliberate, for members of faculty who have committed themselves to this course deliberately chose to place their priorities elsewhere. But if the course were to fail a student in the second group of studies, this would be a serious weakness, and recent changes in the course reflect a concern that theory and practice should mesh better together in precisely these aspects.

One implication of the constraints is that there is rather little scope within two 'university' days for students to be offered a wide range of options on the aspects of the theory which they find most valuable. There is, however, a good deal of such optionality and over the course of the year students may, with an effort on their own part to decide what aspects of study will be most rewarding for them, find that the theory can be to some extent individualised to support practical work and clarify their career aspirations. This is particularly true with regard to the special study but applies for some groups of students to the University work throughout the year as well. Thus on the last two days of each week during *university terms* there is a programme of seminars incorporating the relevant areas of psychology, sociology and values in education, and also the basic skills of literacy and numeracy for those teaching in primary schools. Other parts of these two days are used for films and/or lectures, and for special courses such as sports and games, voice production, creative skills or special education, which are offered on an optional basis.

(3) WHAT IS EXPECTED OF THE STUDENT?

The normal expectation of those who teach in the secondary sector is that each student will go into the school as one of a pair of students from the same discipline. Other PGCE students from different curriculum groups will also be working in the same school. They will be expected to keep school term-times rather than university term-times. They will be given an early opportunity to observe their teacher tutors and other teachers within the schools. Gradually the student will be phased into the teaching situation alongside the teacher tutor, and when the teacher tutor decides that it is appropriate the students will assume full responsibility for a cross-section of classes, both in age and ability. They will normally expect to spend only a part of their time in school in the classroom, the remainder in preparation and other school activities. At different points in the year changes in classes may occur (and be strategically desirable), but the students should have at least one class with whom they are involved for the whole period they are in the school. Students should expect to become involved in out of school activities. They should also be willing to take on relief duties, when the teacher tutor or department colleagues fall sick. They should not be expected to provide relief cover for absent teachers outside the department of their teacher tutor, or, in the case of primary students, the class of their teacher tutor. The students' Thursdays and Fridays are not filled up with lectures, but they are expected to attend the seminars or tutorials that are provided and to use the time available for preparation of materials and reading. From Christmas onwards they will be working on their special study and in the latter part of the course a great deal of their time will be devoted to it.

(4) WHAT IS EXPECTED OF THE TEACHER TUTOR?

The teacher tutors are pivotal figures in our scheme, the anchor person for each student. They are required to lead tutorials for an hour after school not less than once a fortnight or alternatively to contribute with fellow teacher tutors, university colleagues and students to weekly university-based seminars on the teaching of their subject. They write termly reports on their students. This is the minimum programme. But clearly their responsibility to student, at a most vulnerable and critical point in the person's career, far exceeds that description. The pastoral skills of practising teachers are the missing dimension in many conventional forms of teacher training. Given this responsibility, the teacher tutor can carefully select classes in order to give the student variety of experience. They can offer written comments on the students' lesson notes (e.g. exchange from a few years ago – Jenny: 'Terrible class with 3Z today. Out of control – feel like giving up!' Teacher tutor has pencilled in the comment – 'Happens to us all. Happened to me this week on Monday 8 May Period 4'). Indeed the student's lesson notes will often be the basis of the weekly tutorial. They are not 'experts'; so they are not superiors lecturing to inferiors but experienced colleagues working alongside less experienced students in a helping situation. Along with the general tutor they have full responsibility for the assessment of the student as a practising teacher. The general tutor's interim report and the final reports by both tutors are crucial documents in the assessment.

(5) CURRICULUM TUTORS

These are primarily concerned with the study of a preparation for teaching within a particular discipline or an interdisciplinary field. They are responsible for the student's work in his/her curriculum subject, both in the school (along with the teacher tutor) and in the university-based work. They shall keep in close touch with the personal tutor about the general progress of the individual student.

The curriculum tutors take no part in the assessment of the student's teaching; that task has devolved upon skilled practising teachers, individually appointed by the University. The curriculum tutors' task is to give support and guidance in a variety of ways (some organised, some informal or even intangible) to the work of students and teacher tutors, to liaise with them, bring them together in university seminars, and inject from outside the school ideas about innovations in the teachings of the subject.

The curriculum tutor visits the schools normally at least twice in the year, and also receives information from teacher tutors when they visit the University. He/she may be invited to teach in the school as well as to see students teaching, but as a colleague not an assessor. Indeed the student and teacher tutor are deprived of a valuable reinforcement if the curriculum tutor does not visit the school in each term. The curriculum tutor may also play a major part in any curriculum project or research engaged in by either a student or a teacher tutor.

(6) WHY THREE DAYS/TWO DAYS?

Schools would find it easier to timetable in blocks; universities could organize programmes easier in discrete packages; students might find a term in the University and a term in school less disturbing.

We remain unrepentant because of our commitment to a philosophy (see 1) that theory in teacher-training should inter-relate with practice. This entails tension between the two. It is the task of the university faculty and school tutors to try to ensure that the tension does not become insupportable to the student, not that the tension be removed. If the students were only university based in their training, they might be given a vision, but one divorced from reality. If they were totally based in one school for their training, the realism of the experience would be incontestable but they could lose a sense of what was possible outside the walls of the tutorial school. Our course attempts to do both simultaneously; the attempt produces its own kind of tension. But without that challenge none of us – students, teachers and faculty – would want to be committed to our course.

APPENDIX 2

A representative selection of student responses to the PGCE English Course

OPEN LETTER FROM JULIAN

I begin by celebrating the term's work and asking why in heaven's name I've had to wait twenty-five years before reaching a situation where I was encouraged to write creatively out of myself. The workshops have provided a fertile environment for encountering, in many respects for the first time, English as a creative and expressive medium, and have generated ideas and possibilities that have brought exciting and encouraging results in the classroom. I have been genuinely astonished and delighted by the originality and quality of work that children can produce (a reflection of my own paltry experience in the classroom). They have also helped my identification with the classes by putting me through the processes that I would so glibly impose on the children I teach. Maybe teachers should always be expected to do that which they expect their classes to do, to gain some ideas of the difficulties involved. It seems to be of enormous importance to English teachers that this kind of cross fertilization that the workshops provide should be seen as an important part of our resources during our teaching careers, and yet sadly this approach exists in so few schools. The attitude generally appears to be that of allowing teachers to evolve their own techniques and approaches, and not to compromise their 'professional integrity' by suggesting that they might have a lot to contribute to and learn from each other.

The collaboration I have greatly enjoyed, and yet somehow our group has remained composed of individuals. At times it seems that it is only Peter's tireless input that holds us together – the group has not 'gelled', and shows little sign of doing so in the future. Thus we remain colleagues lacking that deeper sense of personal involvement and concern that our shared experience would hopefully produce. But perhaps this is the best sort of preparation for teaching in a society composed of individuals, encouraged by a mechanized culture which allows us to receive all cultural forms at second hand through the media, thus encouraging the growth of the cultural hermit. Perhaps it is simply a reflection of the time it takes to break down the barriers that our classroom experience has taught us to erect. 'Mass culture' whatever it may be, works against spontaneity and creativity because it works against trust and collaboration. If we hope to raise the critical and creative awareness of the children we teach, we have somehow to build trust and collaboration not only in the classroom but in the department and school themselves.

OPEN LETTER FROM JANET: AN EXCERPT

It is astonishing to find the first term over so quickly, and yet, in retrospect, I feel I have gained a great deal from so short a period. For the first two or three workshops I must admit that I suffered from a kind of 'culture-shock'. My previous university background was very different from Sussex, and although I found my new environment far more stimulating and intellectually alive, adapting to the demands of the PGCE course was a gradual process. Later, though, I began to lose self-consciousness and enjoy the workshops, even though on occasions I was unable to write anything. I think the timing of the Thursday sessions may be partly responsible for this, since I have sometimes felt too tired, after three days at school, to give all my energy to the workshops. Thursday afternoon or evening sessions would perhaps be better – at least we would be able to get a little more sleep!

I have found what we actually do increasingly valuable. After the first three workshops I would have liked a more immediately practical session, as I was facing the problem of teaching *Wuthering Heights*, which I admire but do not particularly enjoy, to a fourth year class. I would have liked a workshop dealing with ways of teaching literature and ideas on how to interest rather unwilling kids, as I had few ideas of my own. I think, however, that at the time there were not many others in the group with this problem, and that it was probably better left until this term. Otherwise, I don't have any real criticism of the workshops, apart from the difficulty of finding time to write ballads, etc. amid all the pressures of marking and lesson preparation, which have a tendency to become obsessive if I let them.

Although I am still rather inhibited by my (perhaps) over-developed critical faculty, I am finding the process of writing liberating and, in the highest sense, educational, involving simultaneous exploration of the central object or idea and the total energy and personality of the writer – a genuine expression of the whole person rather than the unemotional, narrow, predetermined track along which so many children are pushed at school. The workshops do, therefore, connect with my experience at school, both in a practical sense – in that the stages of writing and the ways in which ideas have been introduced have directly guided me in some lessons – and in a more ideological sense – in that I am constantly shown the possibilities of a more creative approach in all areas of education.

The workshop on 'frames' has proved invaluable. I was attempting a sort of planning round a theme at the time, and the organization and discussion of a frame really helped to clarify my ideas. In the second term I shall be using two frames, one based on the example of 'man and animals', and involving both class and project work. I also hope to try the idea of the ballad, which could obviously be directly translated for the classroom.

One of the most important features of this course for me is that almost every day I feel that I have developed in some way, either in some teaching skill such as being able to produce lessons which can be fluid enough to follow the way in which the class wants to go, or structuring lessons so that the class can have times of quiet concentration as well as the livelier periods of class discussion or consideration of written material, or on the more conceptual side, dealing with such questions as 'What am I doing? What should I be doing? Where is the system going wrong?' etc.

OPEN LETTER FROM CAROLE: AN EXCERPT

In the first instance I felt wonderfully cleansed by the way everyone succeeded in shedding most of their inhibitions. I felt that force was the only answer and that there was no other way we would have written anything than by being told we *must* write and then we *must* read out what we had written. (I confess I had it very much in my mind to refuse the latter!) Having begun so positively I felt very disappointed when in the third workshop we gave all our time and energies to a discussion of the schools in which we had been placed. I freely admit that, at the time, I wanted and needed this discussion as much as anyone else but, looking back, I feel it was a waste of time in the sense that it was time taken away from the previous act of creating which I desperately wanted to rediscover in myself.

I find it rather paradoxical that I was drawn to this course because of its structure and the amount of time spent in schools and now I feel that purely because of the workshops I feel I would have liked to spend more time in the university. Three and a half hours a week for two terms is just not long enough, perhaps it would be a good idea to have block workshops for two or three days in the last term. I know this is not possible this year but I do feel frustrated in the sense that next term other things must take precedence and personal writing will get lost. I know you might say that we can all carry on writing in our own time and although this is true, that part of me which has been dormant since I was sixteen needs a lot of cajoling, telling and disciplining to revive itself at all. Also the first efforts seem so putrid to my undoubtedly over crititical eye that it will be all too easy to pass over the whole process. All I think I am saying Peter is that I think your workshops are worth far more time than they are given and are of great value as a study in their own right, not something which should have to incorporate lesson plans, discussions of the education system, or indeed anything appertaining to schools. Perhaps a compromise would be for us to spend one month in the university at the beginning of the course, I just don't know.

OPEN LETTER FROM VAL: AN EXCERPT

I think myself that creating ourselves, unashamedly, has been vital; it helps us to understand the need every human being has for *genuine* self-expression and it encouraged us to find a means to release something within ourselves, i.e. our selves, the vital expression. But also it gave us an understanding of the means by which we can encourage this process in children. The vital element towards self-expression seems to me to be the ability to be unashamed, recognizing that our efforts (and, therefore, those of any child who genuinely strives for self-expression) are valid in themselves because they have been *honestly* created by us, because we have allowed them to exist.

I would like to move on now to the idea of risk, the vulnerability of a teacher when she/he cares enough to experiment. To me, there is a very important paradox here, that is, that in experimenting we risk both our own and the class security, we are demanding a lot on trust and yet strangely out of such a risk can come trust, that which we apparently threaten. It seems that only if you are prepared to step beyond the safe boundaries can you really get to know the 'hidden' part of your class, the more personal and private side of children. Their reactions, comments and finally their contributions through their written work reveal, I think, more in an apparently 'risky' lesson than a term of 'safe' ones.

The idea of daring to try something new or different, of taking a risk appealed to me. Although I dreaded my vulnerability, there was something in the risk that I found intoxicating. Your first workshop could have fallen apart if we had not been so well trained! (You admitted you were bothered by the reaction of what you proposed.) Without becoming 'teacher's pet' I would like to thank you for that first workshop. Experimenting has become a vital part of my nascent relationship with 4Ti, even if they do 'fight back'!

So I do understand 'the wanting and not wanting' to try an idea, but 'wanting' wins because new experiences are intoxicating, and I am learning a lot from them.

OPEN LETTER FROM JOANNA: AN EXCERPT

I'd like to make a few, general comments, before moving on to cover the major points raised in your letters. I eventually overcame my dread of our Thursday morning sessions. First they were an education in sharing, trusting and feeling unintimidated within a university, which was not a feature of my undergraduate experience. Also, they were a strain on my energy and enthusiasm, nine-thirty in the morning is a difficult time at which to feel coherent, let alone creative! The schizophrenia of the course, also dictated that I felt guilty at not having enough time and energy to devote myself wholeheartedly sometimes, to the workshop sessions.

I don't actually share your opinion that we have cohered as a group. We are a bunch of strong-willed and strong-minded individuals and we have occasionally been collaborators. Trust amongst us has developed, yet I think it is perhaps time to see us in action as teachers, albeit in a contrived workshop setting (one of your ideas last term).

The quotation 'I know because I have done' should be qualified by 'and have shared' and these are essential sentiments for me to hold, to prevent myself becoming a fraudulent teacher. The dictum, 'I want you to be selfish', something I shared, led me straight into the gulf which separates school from university seminars. I have started pottery at school, to the accusation by my general tutor of selfishness, 'you're not here for yourself, you know'. Amazing conflicts prevail!

Our training and conditioning are still barriers to sharing, however I feel I have personally progressed and benefitted from the workshop sessions. The critically evaluative and over-conceptual side of my nature has, perhaps blocked the creative and expressive in the past. Hence my reactions to my own poem, 'Frost'. The expressive versus the conceptual has been the biggest conflict inherent in the workshops. It still has not been satisfactorily examined. However, the inward revelation, gained last term, has at last halted my endless battling with King's College and all it stood for in my mind. The conflict of approaches reveals itself in the steering of our sessions in certain directions by various individuals. We still fall over ourselves to over-conceptualize.

Another area of conflict is the constraint operating on us, within our schools. The ceaseless demand on my time and my own desire to be an energetic and committed English teacher, makes me place emphasis on the school-side of the course. You speak of us imbibing judgement along the lines of right/wrong, pass/fail, yet we're teaching kids who aren't present in the classroom of their own volition and who constantly hold up work saying, "I've finished. Is it good? Do you like it?" This course is run on a pass/fail basis too. Much of the time we are forced to work within constraints of an examination system, with kids who have been conditioned to expect competitive grading. It is hard to begin to break down these barriers, yet essential. I feel at times to be in the re-educating business, a doubly heavy task!

OPEN LETTER FROM JIM: AN EXCERPT

The sessions stand out as apart from school, i.e. very different – but also highly relevant and related to classroom practice, as a consideration of the nature of our work in school. The sessions are thus made more vital by being firmly placed in the context of the whole week, and not just the 'University side' of the course.

I believe it is the workshop sessions that have really kept me thinking during this term – obviously the work in school demands thought, analysis, discussion etc., but it also needs a framework which the Thursday morning helps provide. This framework is based upon a literary philosophy, thus those who have most to say to us from the past are 'literary philosophers' themselves, Coleridge, Nietzsche, Yeats . . . .

Yeats, for example, is superbly valuable in our discovering such a framework – but for his literary insights and craft, not for his philosophy. Which is not to say that the only really valuable poetry is necessarily philosophical, or that only philosophers who are also fine literary artists 'matter', or are truly great. To broaden out this idea: Yeats said that: 'Art is a vision of reality' – thus we could say that to an extent all literature is philosophical, but we also need the philosophy of a Coleridge or a Nietzsche to clarify, define and strengthen our argument and standpoint.

Thus I would argue with your presentation of a literary heritage that supports your own philosophy, running from Blake through Coleridge, Wordsworth, Keats, Carlyle, Arnold, Ruskin, Morris, Lawrence, Eliot, Leavis, Holbrook, to us in the University of Sussex on Thursday mornings. My point, and it is not 'academic', is that these people do not represent a common tradition except in the loosest and vaguest manner imaginable. They all said different things, that is obvious, but they do not agree on fundamental basics either, to make them do so is to lose the vital elements of those who really have something to say. Thus I cannot see that to say – this is I'm afraid a parody – that we are all part of a living culture, stressing 'imagination' or demonstrating true 'existentialism' serves any purpose other than to strip imagination and existentialism of any meaning altogether other than as 'hurrah' words, opposed to Locke, James Mill, empiricism and utilitarianism in general, – 'boo' words . . . .

Process is only achieved through a dynamic tension and conflict, as between the Apollinian and Dionysian in Nietzsche's *Birth of tragedy*. Our expressiveness must itself be disciplined. You say that when we write poetry, to begin with, all thoughts must come uncensored out on to the page – surely this cannot be so. Our whole life is an expressive act, or series of acts, of sublimation. Too far in such a 'free' spontaneous method, approach, lies chaos, not a Nietzschian 'dancing star'! We must not inhibit, or quell, worthwhile ideas, flows of thought in ourselves or our pupils – but there is also a place for a mask or a discipline that leads on to a finer creativity – and a finer creation; a conscious shaping of the artefact and the artist.

One way we grow is through encountering art, experiencing the finished yet living artefact. Is reading Donne, Yeats, etc., any the less creative than writing a poem yourself?

They are different – but neither less valuable; both are expressive, disciplined, shaping activities. Nietzsche talks of art in terms of received artefacts *and* creative experience – ours as well as the author's.

OPEN LETTER FROM PAULINE: AN EXCERPT

I suggested earlier that as a child increases his command of the language of an arts subject (i.e. his knowledge and command of words, the uses and combinations of colour and line, musical notes, the expressive capacities of the body, etc.) he increases his potential to express himself through the medium of that subject in terms which will convey his experience accurately to his audience. The greater the artist's knowledge of his tools and of the forms and styles in which they can be used the greater the likelihood, I would suggest, of him being able to symbolise his experience in terms which will enable an audience to perceive the essence of that experience. Thus, the greater the child's command of vocabulary, the greater his powers of expression. This is one of the reasons why I feel that you have neglected in your letters and in the workshops the fact that an extremely important function of English teaching is simply language development.

I am in full sympathy with a statement which you made in the first letter and have continued to defend:

It is in the nature of human nature that it desires to express itself, to give shape to its experience so that it can simultaneously posses itself and transmit itself to others.

However, in order to do any of this, a child must have the words at his fingertips with which he can conceptualise his experience. Not until then can he either possess it or transmit it to others. You also stress the importance of introducing the English student to the great works of his cultural heritage without mentioning, as I think I would, that language development is an essential prerequisite for the interpretation of such writings. Would you agree that the prime importance of such literature is its content which provides us with bases upon which to evaluate our own experience rather than the form and style in which it is written?

I would suggest that alongside lessons based specifically upon the encouragement and development of creative writing should be lessons based specifically upon language development and the understanding of language, from contemporary society and from past cultures. Words, being our commonest form of communication are constantly abused and misused so that their true definitions are often lost amidst a complex muddle of loose associations. Many good examples of misuse might be found in the mouth of that enemy of yours the 'Counterfeit Culture'. It is also generally acknowledged that words are commonly perverted in the cause of political propaganda. You recognise both these facts in *Root and blossom*. An important aim of the language syllabus could be to redefine words by tracing them back to their roots in a manner similar to that suggested by Herbert Kohl in *36 Children*:

Actually it was the study of language and myth, of the origins and history of words, of their changing uses and functions in human life.

From this, one might go on to introduce new concepts such as: *moral, irony, superficial, faith, doubt*, that might help a child to define his experience and to understand it. Kohl's pupils expressed this need spontaneously:

Not content to be fed solely words that grew from sources that I the teacher presented, they asked for words that fitted unnamed and partially articulated concepts they had, or situations they couldn't adequately describe.

Wesker, in his essay 'Words as Definitions of Experience' argues the need for equipping the child with a basic vocabulary of key concepts which are an essential prerequisite for the ethical ordering of experience and would consequently provide a degree of protection against 'mindless violence, political tyranny, spiritual and emotional exploitation'. Believing words to be of paramount importance in the understanding of ourselves and the world in which we live, he is surprised that there is not already a subject on the curriculum devoted to the study of words, with a title like 'definitions of experience'. His argument is summed up in the following statement with which I fully sympathise:

> If education means anything, it means essentially this: the upholding of language as man's greatest creation. It means a constant freshening, a constant guarding against abuse by demagogues, bureaucrats and copy writers, whether political or commercial.

If such lessons could be used to sharpen our minds, and our children's minds; if we were better equipped with a vocabulary of concepts with which to understand the subtleties of our experience, should we not be better equipped for the attempts to express, possess and transmit this experience to others?

There is not an awful lot I want to say about the workshops at the moment, except that I have felt very annoyed at times by the huge contradiction between my teaching experience and my 'workshop' experience! However much I like it, I am having to teach large classes and, consequently, all my energy is spent in developing techniques of keeping them in control in order that they are in a position to learn. Until I have fully mastered this craft I cannot even begin to think about how I can contribute to the personal development of each individual in any meaningful way. We are all at a crisis point with our strengths of discipline being mercilessly tested and for this initial period we have *got* to concern ourselves with trivialities such as how to let the class enter the room. After we have come to terms with the existing *realities* of the classes we teach and the schools in which we teach, then might we be able to concentrate more fully upon how we can apply our 'creative intentions' to the situations in which we find ourselves. We have to learn to float before we can swim!

OPEN LETTER FROM MARY: AN EXCERPT

Yes, we came through – many of us exhausted mentally and physically. I had gone through times of frustration, anger, despair and anxiety as well as interest, excitement, enjoyment, enthusiasm and even elation. I found the workshops fascinating, frightening, irritating and sometimes irrelevant. For example the demand made to write creatively and imaginatively put an enormous pressure on me. I've always felt I could not write, that other people can describe and express things so much better than I can. Nevertheless, I can understand the importance of trying to write myself, if I am going to make such demands on a class of school children. I was fascinated to see if I could write anything worthwhile; I was frightened at being exposed – being asked to hand something in to be judged by someone else and having my work put in front of our group for evaluative comments. Somehow it made me feel vulnerable – everyone would see what rubbish I write, what a lack of imagination I have. How could I think that I could teach English?! I was also irritated by the discussions that seemed to go on too long, where one or two members of the group seemed to dominate the discussion, take it the way they wanted it to go and monopolise the workshop time; and I sometimes found the idealism and the discussion irrelevant.

What have I drawn out for myself from the collaborative sessions of making (in the case of the ballad and the frames, for example) and evaluation? I enjoyed making the ballad. It was fun. At first I felt the ballad form was undermining the tragedy of the event. The way we composed it, trying to make rhymes and compose in such a very simple, and perhaps hackneyed, form seemed too lighthearted and unfeeling. However, it was fun to do and when I heard the finished results – heard them read onto the tape-recorder, I was so impressed. Out of this rather jocular approach had come some sensitive, moving ballads. I realised how important the presentation of the work was – the way the ballads were read was most important. I like the idea of frames and I found the frames of the other students very helpful. I still keep trying to work out frames for myself but I do not get very far with them. I find they take a long time to prepare and I cannot find the time because lesson planning takes me so long. However, I feel that when I am working from a frame, then the lesson planning and the frame preparation will link together. Last term I was doing more individually planned lessons. I am not too sure about the work we did on evaluation. I am not so convinced about the common criteria for critical evaluation of poetry. I felt that in our sessions the common criticisms were somewhat forced; that we were all trying to find them and striving to give the answer that our teacher wanted. Maybe the common criteria were there and I am taking the fact that I did not always agree with the evaluation as a sign that common criteria do not exist. Nevertheless, I got the feeling, when Peter summed up our critical statements about the poems that he selected the comments and statements, that supported his belief in common criteria.

What connections are you able to make between the workshop and the classrooms in which you are now busily teaching? I have already answered this question to some extent. I feel that I was not able to make very strong connections between the workshops and the classroom. The two situations seemed poles apart and put entirely different demands on me. However, there are connections and the main one for me is the value of trying to do what I shall so often be asking my children to do – write creatively.

OPEN LETTER FROM MAXINE: AN EXCERPT

You will appreciate that any report on a term's work will necessarily concentrate on the gap between school and our meetings at Sussex University, which is the space in which we as student teachers must operate a shuttle between. Rightly or wrongly our assessment of the volume of what we have been doing will tend to focus on the effectiveness with which we can apply what we have been doing to the classroom situation – even though that activity is not necessarily directed towards 'effectiveness'.

My own attitude is more complex because I did not necessarily envisage the course only as a period of practical training but saw it as presenting an opportunity for personal development and growth. Consequently I have found perhaps unfairly that the course has not functioned particularly well on either level, for although I believe that many of the tasks you have set us have been interesting and stimulating, they seem to have been intended to address us not so much as adult individuals in our own right or as prospective teachers but to place us in the situation of the child and, more specifically, in the position of a child who cannot question – so to this extent it seems difficult to comment on the course at all.

At the same time I have found some of the exercises you have given us to do very useful in the classroom situation. In particular the projects of writing a ballad about the Rye Harbour disaster and the ideas you have on myths and monsters which have stimulated and captured the imagination of the children. But precisely because these exercises worked so well with some children I was at the same time forced to recognise that there are major obstacles standing in the way of a successful realisation of such creative projects as far as many other children are concerned. For they are often held back by the limitations of their own vocabulary by the fact that they have often read little that would stimulate their own imagination and because they lack either the experience or the willingness to enter fully into the spirit of something which lies beyond the range of their normal experience. I do not believe that the general attitude of a school like Beacon where there is an extreme reluctance to use books in any context can be of much help but there is more generally the problem of knowing what to do about work that is half-hearted, unimaginative and incomplete. Are the children to be blamed for not doing better, has the teacher failed to successfully communicate her vision? Is the whole environment of school, home and television one which militates against creativity and self-expression? Or is self-expression a more difficult goal than we are often disposed to imagine? All these are questions that have passed through my mind in the course of the term's work.

Particularly with my 'lower range ability' classes I have found a tendency in the children to turn even the most interesting project into a dreary, mechanical piece of work which they approach in much the same spirit as if they were asked to copy out the same sentence a hundred times. Perhaps this is not really unexpected – to use one's imagination is obviously hard work, which, fairly predictably they stay away from. But this also indicates that 'spontaneity', a notion so beloved by educationalists, can not altogether be relied upon.

Undoubtedly lack of experience, in the sense of a wide fund of experiences to draw upon, is a major stumbling block for many children when it comes to writing, the more so because they have not been encouraged to reflect on things that have happened to them. Therefore I feel that to present children with a succession of creative projects may become sterile and exhausting. They need to read more and expose themselves more to the experiences of others if there is to be a basis for their own imaginative activities.

OPEN LETTER FOR MY TUTOR FROM SIMON: AN EXCERPT

There are two things I want to say in beginning this letter. The first is that I take the word open in a very serious sense. I intend this letter to be as honest and as direct as possible. The second is that I have called you my tutor – this is important for me. I am a student and you are my tutor. I sense from the way in which you have asked us to write you a letter that you are asking for a clear individual response to your seminars in the way that you have given us a response to the way you see the seminars. I will try to do this. I have begun with these two statements because I sense that what you are asking for is in a way impossible. You have asked us for our views honestly, but we are your students, and you are our tutor. I think therefore it is only possible for us to answer your questions as students. The same problem appears in a classroom. There, roles are reversed, we are the teachers and we are faced with a class of students. Unfortunately, here I have to address myself to the class as students. I cannot speak directly to them as individuals. The structure of the system does not allow this. In the same way, you as a teacher cannot speak directly to us, your students, because the structure of the system does not allow it. I think that teachers are like animals in cages. Occasionally we see a gap in the bars that appears large enough to squeeze through but on close inspection there is never enough room to get through. I pass you this letter with these thoughts in mind. An open letter perhaps is a way of smuggling something through the bars unnoticed . . . .

I think it is important to realise that writing poetry is part of us. It is like the clothes we wear, disorganised, dishevelled, colourful, drab, boring, original, artistic. We should learn to look at our poetry as part of ourselves just as we should learn to look at the way we dress. It is us, as we are, and we should learn to be ourselves instead of simply acting out ourselves. A lot of your work with poetry, literature and education applies itself to this area and I think it is an area, like a forest, that is impossible to discover completely, but is very deep and full of things to experience.

Your comment about teaching as an art form is also interesting. Teaching should be part of yourself. It should be creative and spontaneous. In this sense it is an art form and I agree with you. But what record can it leave? Surely the best teaching is invisible – it means doing nothing. Children surely teach themselves, we are there to hold up the mirror so that they can see themselves but ideally they should be able to take down their own pocket mirror and use it all the time. I believe a lot of children do this anyway, which is why they are exciting and honest. Adults become strange. They don't like to take out the mirror too often – it disturbs them; they prefer to look at other people and take comfort in the fact that they do not look like that. So when you say teaching is an art form I agree. The art, I think, is to disappear completely – this is not possible in a class, the structure puts you in front of a class and *makes* you the teacher but I think this goal is worth working toward.

But yes, I agree, teaching is elusive; it leaves no record except for the register. I agree, too, that poetry is an enactment. The words on the page are you. People should be trained to keep diaries, to write things down. It is a simple form of therapy. People have feelings they cannot cope with. There are often many times when these things weigh you down like giant sandbags strapped round your waist. Our way to help the problem is first to see that you have it. This means seeing that you are weighed down. If you write down your thoughts they become clear for you to see. And sometimes admitting to yourself that there is a problem is enough to make the sandbags dissolve and you can begin to walk again. Poetry and writing is therefore a very powerful force – a doctor, nurse and friend. Prose is not enough.

I also want to criticise you because if I do that, it puts my thoughts in a clearer perspective. You talked in the same seminar about dialogue, tension and process and you spoke about 'existential accuracy'. A politician is someone who finds a vocabulary to match his creed. The vocabulary becomes a pair of crutches without which he cannot walk. My criticism would, therefore, be that you do not need the words 'existential accuracy' to communicate to us your sense of poetry. Words are very strange things, they often confuse rather than illuminate.

AN OPEN LETTER FROM FRED: AN EXCERPT

I see man as active in his creativity. I see him as a being potentially able to form hypotheses which he can subject to deductive reasoning; capable of theory testing which results in an existential level of meaning in Witkin's terms. The greater the variety and complexity of hypotheses that he can generate, the more is he likely to be considered creative; and part of this creativity will also be his 'feeling' in regard to the components of his hypothesis. This feeling is not a passive or emotional reaction to the given components. It has been actively formed through a deductive analysis in conjunction with other stored results of past 'hypothesis testing'. As Witkin says: 'Feeling is quite distinct from mood or emotion. It is the reflexive component of the affective life. It is the fabric of Being'.

It seems to me that the implications of accepting this approach are very important in my practice. It must involve presenting situations to the child which he is able to prepare hypotheses on (or to 'reciprocate' with the situation in Witkin's terms). These situations must be within the capacity of the child's ability to bridge the gap between his conceptualisation of past experience and the present hypothesis that is required in order to understand it.

As I see it, the practical classroom implications of this personal interpretation of Witkin are to stress the importance of using experiences that the child has actually lived through, rather than those recreated by verbal and written forms. But once the 'raw material' has been experienced, this then can be subjected to a profound refinement and sophisticated analysis in terms of its definition in written form.

AN OPEN LETTER FROM HEATHER: AN EXCERPT

I have often found that the best way to test the validity of a particular thesis is to attempt to find loopholes in an argument, pursue them to their logical conclusion and then, with the benefit of further reflection, examine whether there are *really* any areas where the thesis in question cannot be applied. In trying to argue against the Abbsian view of English teaching and in being defeated on every point of contention that I attempted to find, I feel I have made the best possible personal vindication of your views. By attempting to rebel against your ideas I have tested their strength in every educational area I can think of. As a result, I have not little or nothing to say against the theoretical framework which has been presented in the first term of the curriculum meetings. But I am now much more convinced of its applicability to all areas of English teaching than I would have been if I had merely accepted your ideas wholesale in the first place. Testing them out in my teaching practice has, of course, also helped me a great deal. It has given them the practical backing which they lacked at the beginning of term. At that stage, I simply had a tacit acceptance of what you were trying to put over.

However, there have been problems for me in the first term and I do not think I have been alone in encountering them. In the first open letter, you urged us to be selfish about the workshops and to ask ourselves what we could personally get out of them. Now teaching, it seems to me, is an extraordinarily and perhaps uniquely 'other'-orientated profession. Hence, for the first three days of each week, I have found myself thrust into as deep a consideration of the needs, abilities and aspirations of others as I can manage and I have found the switch to 'self'-orientation on Thursday mornings almost impossible to make. Even the creativity involved in lesson planning is decidely 'other' orientated and has nothing to do with the pure creativity, from the self/for the self, that we have been urged to engage in during the workshops.

APPENDIX 3

Towards a More Sensitive 'A' Level Literature Examination

The following key excerpts have been taken from the 1979 document *Proposal for a syllabus in English literature at 'A' level with a component of internally-assessed course work* released by the Associated Examining Board. This pioneering examination represents a significant move towards a more sensitive 'A' level paper. Once this new examination has been widely adopted (as it deserves to be) the next step for teachers accepting the concept of English as an expressive discipline would be to include as an intrinsic part of the course, a strong element of expressive work.

AIMS AND OBJECTIVES

(1) To extend the range of English studies in the sixth form and, whilst retaining critical essay on a set text, to give the opportunity for more varied work.
(2) To widen the reading of 'A' level students beyond a limited number of set texts.
(3) To enable the student to pursue in greater depth a particular interest in literature, whilst ensuring that he also reads major writer's work.
(4) To encourage the student to work steadily throughout the course in the knowledge that his course-work will count towards his final result.
(5) To give the student an opportunity to work under conditions which scholars would regard as essential, i.e. with access to texts and reference work and without a time-limit of forty five minutes or an hour for a unit of work.
(6) To provide an opportunity for the teacher to participate in the assessment of students' work and to have experience of assessment procedures.
(7) To increase the probability that the assessment accurately reflects the work done during the course.
(8) To obtain and assess a wider and more varied sample of the student's work in English.
(9) To maintain comparability with other 'A' level syllabuses by allocating the majority of marks to an externally set and marked examination but at the same time to provide an opportunity for individual choice in a substantial part of the syllabus.

SYLLABUS CONTENT

The syllabus will include comprehension and practical criticism, prescribed texts by Shakespeare, a long poem or not more than four poems of moderate length, major playwrights and major novelists together with an anthology of poetry. These sections of the syllabus would be externally examined, leaving schools and colleges to propose their own lists of texts or other aspects of English studies subject to the approval of the Board.

The lay-out of the papers would be:

Paper 1 (3 hours) Two passages for comprehension and practical criticism, one prose and one poetry. Candidates would be expected to show an understanding of content, themes and development together with a sensitive response to mood, atmosphere, language and rhythm, and the appropriateness of the form to the content. On one passage candidates might be asked to express their own views on a topic mentioned in the passage. In addition, candidates would be required to answer a question on a poem or poems from the anthology. Candidates would have access to the text or texts, so enabling them to provide a critical response in some depth with close reference to the poems. A choice of question may be given.

Paper 2 (3 hours) Candidates would be required to answer four questions, one on a Shakespeare play, one on a long poem or not more than four poems of moderate length, (Chaucer or Pope or Browning or Milton or another poet), one on a play, and one on a novel. In each case there would be a choice from three options (e.g. a novel by Fielding or

Jane Austen or Hardy). There will be a choice from two questions on each prescribed text. Some of the questions may provide a substantial passage from the text as a starting-point. The questions should be framed so that they are capable of being answered *in forty five minutes*. They should emphasise critical response rather than memorisation and should be specific rather than general essays. Access to the texts of the plays and poems should be allowed.

Coursework Schools and colleges will choose a minimum of six texts other than those prescribed for paper 2. These will include a Shakespeare play and a non-fictional prose work. Choices will be subject to the approval of the Board. Each candidate will compile a folder of eight units of coursework of an average length of about 800 words. At least one unit will be written on each of the six texts. A review of a theatrical performance of a play seen by the candidate, in which the production is related to the text, will be acceptable as one unit; the review should consider how far the production satisfactorily realises what is in the text, and in what ways it illuminates the text beyond the potentialities word alone.

The coursework will also include one extended essay of about 3,000 words on a broader basis than a single text. The subject may be a genre within a period, (e.g. the treatment of the Crucifixion in medieval plays); a theme (comparison of 'Utopias'); several works by one writer (e.g. Graham Greene's novels with tropical settings). The extended essay may arise from the study of a prescribed text or a book chosen for course-work, but should not be exclusively concerned with this book.

FORM OF ASSESSMENT

The two examination papers will be sent and the marking will be co-ordinated by an examiner appointed by the Board. It is hoped that some assistant examiners can be appointed from tutors preparing students for the examination, but tutors will not mark the work of their own students. This appointment will give tutors experience of assessment procedures, standards and criteria. The experience will be useful in assessing coursework and should provide a means of improving comparability between assessments in different schools and colleges. Marking and awarding procedures will follow the same pattern as the Board's Mode 1 examinations with a detailed marking-scheme, exchanges of scripts, sampling of scripts by the Chief Examiner, adjustments of individual marks, statistical analyses of papers, award meeting for fixing grade boundaries, and review of awards.

The employment of tutors as examiners would have a number of advantages. It would create and maintain interest in the syllabus amongst both students and tutors; it would train teachers in the rudiments of assessment techniques; it would provide an opportunity for discussion of matters of professional interest; it would give a clearer notion of criteria and standards of assessment of English at this level, which would be carried over to the assessment of coursework.

Mark-allocations are:

Paper 1 Three questions, two comprehension-practical criticism, one question on a poem or poems from the set anthology. Forty marks for each question. Total 120 marks.

Paper 2 Four questions, one on each of four books. Thirty marks for each question. Total 120 marks.

Coursework Ten marks for each of eight units plus forty marks for the extended essay. Total 120 marks.

Total marks for the whole examination: 360 marks.

The coursework will be internally assessed by tutors and will be subject to moderation by moderators appointed by the Board. It is proposed to arrange workshops for tutors with moderators presiding in each of the areas where the examination will be held. At these workshops samples of coursework will be discussed in detail and assessed. The discussion will identify the causes of any differences in assessment and enable moderators to give guidance leading to comparability of assessment between centres. The Chief Examiner will act as moderator to one area group and will attend the workshops in other areas to ensure comparability between the groups. A sample of about five folders from each centre should be extracted for the award stage. It will then be possible to produce correlations for each group and each centre between written papers and coursework. Any apparent inconsistency can be investigated so that it can be satisfactorily accounted for, or adjustments to the marking can be made to bring the centres and groups into line with each other.

In papers 1 and 2 candidates will be permitted to take texts of prescribed poems and plays, but not novels, into the examination room. More important, since the kind of question one can ask in an open-book examination is different from what an examiner asks for in a traditional examination, tutors will need to consider the effects of this type of examination on their preparation of candidates. The emphasis will presumably be greater on critical response, less on memorisation.

SELECT BIBLIOGRAPHY 1

On Expressive Disciplines, Culture and Education

Abbs, P. (ed.) *The black rainbow*. Heinemann Educational Books, 1975
  Autobiography in education. Gryphon Press, 1977
  Reclamations. Heinemann Educational Books, 1979
Abbs, P. and Carey, G. *Proposal for a new college*. Heinemann Educational Books, 1977
Arnheim,R. *Towards a psychology of art*. Faber and Faber
Arnold, M. *Culture and anarchy*. Cambridge University Press, 1932
  Essays in criticism, University of Chicago Press, 1969
Auty, G. *The art of deception*. Libertarian Books, 1977
Bantock, G. H. *Education, culture and the emotions*. Faber and Faber, 1967
  Education in an industrial society. Faber and Faber, 1973
Barrett, W. *Irrational man*. Heinemann Educational Books, 1977
Berger, J. *Ways of seeing*. Penguin, 1972
Berlin, I. *Vico and Herder*. Hogarth Press, 1976
Buber, M. *Between man and man*. Fontana, 1961
  I and thou T. and T. Clark, 1971
Carlyle, T. *Signs of the time*
Campbell, J. *Primitive mythology*. Souvenir Press, 1973
  Oriental Mythology. Souvenir Press, 1973
  Myths to live by. Souvenir Press, 1973
  Occidental Mythology. Souvenir Press, 1974
Cassirer, E. *Essay on man*. Yale University Press, 1944
  The philosophy of symbolic forms in 3 volumes. Yale University Press, 1953, 1955, 1958
Coleridge, S. T. *Biographia literaria*. Dent, 1975
Collingwood, R. G. *The principles of art*. Oxford University Press, 1958
Eliot, T. S. *Notes towards the difinition of culture*. Faber and Faber, 1948
Erikson, E. *Childhood and society*. Paladin, 1977
Frankl, V. *Psychotherapy and existentialism*. Penguin, 1973
Friedman, M. *The worlds of existentialism*. University of Chicago Press, 1973
Fromm, E. *To have or to be*. Jonathan Cape, 1978
Frye, N. *The stubborn structure*. Methuen, 1970
  The modern century. Oxford University Press, 1968
Grant, G. *Technology and empire*. Anansi, 1969
  Time as history. Canadian Broadcasting Corporation, 1969
Grene, M. *The knowee and the known*. University of California Press, 1974
Harding, D. W. *Experience into words*. Penguin.
Harding, R. *Anatomy of inspiration*, F. Cass, 1967
Hegel, G. W. F. *The phenomenology of mind*. Allen and Unwin, 1931
Henry, J. *Culture against man*. Penguin, 1972
Hillman *Emotion* Routledge and Kegan Paul, 1960
  Revisioning psychology Harper Torchbooks, 1975
Hirst, P. H. and Peters *The logic of education*. Routledge and Kegan Paul, 1970
Hodges, H. A. *The Philosophy of Wilhelm Dilthey*. Greenwood Press, 1952
Holbrook, D. *Human hope and the death instinct*. Pergamon, 1971
  Gustav Mahler and the courage to be. Vision Press, 1975
Hourd, M. *Relationship in learning*. Heinemann Educational Books, 1972
Hudson, L. *Contrary imaginations*. Penguin, 1968
  The cult of the fact. Jonathan Cape, 1972
  Human beings. Jonathan Cape, 1975

Inglis, F. *The imagery of power*. Heinemann Educational Books, 1972
  Ideology and the imagination. Cambridge University Press, 1975
Jones, D. *Epoch and artist*. Faber and Faber, 1973
Jones, R. M. *Fantasy and feeling in education*. New York University Press, 1968
Jung, C. G. *Symbols of transformation*. Routledge and Kegan Paul, 1956
  The archetypes and the collective unconscious. Routledge and Kegan Paul, 1959
  Memories, dreams, reflections. Fontana, 1967
Kant, I. *Critique of pure reason*. Dent, 1969
  Critique of Judgement. Oxford University Press, 1978
Kaufmann, W. (ed) *Existentialism from Dostoevsky to Sartre*. Meridian Books, 1977
Kierkegaard, S. *Either/Or* Anchor Books, 1959
Koestler A. *The act of creation*. Picador, 1975
Laing, R. D. *The divided self*. Penguin, 1970
Langer, S. *Feeling and form*. Routledge and Kegan Paul, 1953
  Philosophy in a new key. Harvard University Press, 1957
  Mind: an essay on human feeling. Johns Hopkins University Press, 1974
Lawrence, D. H. *Selected Essays*. Penguin, 1950
  Fantasia of the Unconscious and Psychoanalysis and the Unconscious. Penguin, 1971
Leavis, F. R. *Education and the university*. Chatto and Windus, 1965
  Nor shall my sword. Chatto and Windus, 1972
  The living principle. Chatto and Windus, 1975
  Thought, words and creativity. Chatto and Windus, 1976
Lomas, P. *True and false Experience*. Allen Lane/The Penguin Press, 1973
Macmurray, J. *The self as agent*. Faber and Faber, 1957
  Reason and emotion. Faber and Faber, 1935
  Persons in relation. Faber and Faber, 1961
Marcuse, H. *One-dimensional man*. Sphere Books, 1972
Marshall, S. *An experiment in education*. Cambridge University Press, 1966
McLuhan, M. *The Gutenburg galaxy*. Routledge and Kegan Paul, 1967
Mill, J. S. *Autobiography*. Oxford University Press, 1971
  On Bentham and Coleridge. Cambridge University Press, 1966
Milner, M. *On not being able to paint*. Heinemann Educational Books, 1971
Morris, W. (ed Morton, A. L.) *Political writings*. Lawrence and Wishart, 1973
Mumford, L. *Art and technics*. Columbia University Press, 1952
  The transformations of man. Allen and Unwin, 1957
  The city in history. Secker and Warburg, 1961
  The myth of the machine in 2 volumes. Secker and Warburg
Murdoch, I. *The fire and the sun*. Oxford University Press, 1978
Newman *The idea of a University*. Oxford University Press, 1976
Niblett, W. R. (ed) *The sciences, the humanities and the Technological Threat*.
  University of London Press, 1975
Nietzsche, F. *On the birth of tragedy*. Vintage Books, 1967
  The will to power. Vintage Books, 1973
  Untimely meditations
Ortega Y Gasset, J. *The revolt of the masses*. Allen and Unwin, 1961
  The dehumanization of art. Princeton University Press, 1968
Peters, R. S. *Psychology and ethical development*. Allen and Unwin, 1974
Phenix, P. H. *Realms of Meaning*. McGraw Hill, 1964
Plato *The republic*. Penguin, 1970
Polanyi, M. *Personal Knowledge*. Routledge and Kegan Paul, 1973
Poole, R. *Towards Deep Subjectivity*. Allen Lane/The Penguin Press, 1972
Read, H. *Redemption of the robot*. Faber and Faber, 1970
  The forms of things unknown. Faber and Faber, 1960

The grassroots of art. Faber and Faber, 1955
Ikon and idea. Faber and Faber, 1955
Reid, L. A. *Meaning in the arts.* Allen and Unwin.
Ways of knowledge and experience. Allen and Unwin.
Richards/I. A. *Principles of literary criticism.* Routledge and Kegan Paul, 1926
Richards, M. *Centring.* Wesleyan University Press, 1979
Richard, M. *Art and the child.* University of London.
Rieff, P. *Fellow teachers.* Faber and Faber, 1975
The triumph of the therapeutic. Penguin, 1973
Robertson, S. *Rosegarden and labyrinth.* Gryphon Press, 1982
Robinson, I. *The survival of English.* Cambridge University Press, 1974
Ross, M. *The creative arts.* Heinemann Educational Books, 1978
Arts and the adolescent. HMSO, 1980
Roszak, T. *Where the wasteland ends.* Faber and Faber, 1973
Rousseau, J. J. *Emile.* Dent, 1974
Sapir, E. *Culture, language and personality.* University of California Press, 1956
Sartre, J. P. *Sketch for a theory of the emotions.* Methuen, 1971
Being and nothingness, Methuen, 1969
Schiller, F. *On the aesthetic education of man.* Oxford, 1974
Shelley, P. B. *An essay on poetry,* 1821
Small, C. *Music, society, education.* John Calder, 1978
Steiner, G. *Language and Silence.* Penguin, 1967
Heidegger. Fontana, 1978
Storr, A. *Dynamics of creation.* Secker and Warburg, 1972
Thompson, D. *Discrimination and popular culture.* Penguin, 1970
Walsh, W. *The use of imagination.* Chatto and Windus, 1959
Warnock, M. *Imagination.* Faber and Faber, 1980
Whyte, L. L. *The unconscious before Freud.* Tavistock Publications, 1962
Williams, R. *Communications.* Penguin, 1970
Culture and society. Penguin, 1971
The long revolution. Penguin, 1961
Winnicot, D. W. *Playing and reality.* Tavistock Publications, 1971
Witkin, R. *The intelligence of feeling.* Heinemann Educational Books, 1974
Wordsworth *Preface to lyrical ballads.* Greenwood Press, 1979

SELECT BIBLIOGRAPHY 2

On English Teaching

Abbs, P. *English for diversity*. Heinemann Educational Books, 1969
  Root and blossom. Heinemann Educational Books, 1976
Allen, D. *English teaching Since 1965*. Heinemann Educational Books, 1980
Barnes, D. and Todd, F. *Language, the learner and the school*. Penguin, 1969
Bernstein, B. *Class, codes and control* in 3 volumes. Routledge and Kegan Paul, 1977, 1973 and 1977
Britton, J. *Language and learning*. Penguin, 1972
Calthrop, K. *Reading together*. Heinemann Educational Books, 1973
Cook, C. *The play way*. London, 1917.
Cook, E. *The ordinary and the fabulous*. Cambridge, 1976
Couch, Q. *On the art of writing*. Cambridge.
Creber, J. W. P. *Sense and sensitivity*. University of London Press, 1965
  Lost for words. Penguin, 1972
Dixon, J. *Growth through English*. Oxford University Press, 1975
Druce, R. *The eye of innocence*. University of London Press, 1970
Harrison, B. *An arts-based approach to English studies*. Hodder and Stoughton, 1982
Holbrook, D. *English for the rejected*. Cambridge University Press, 1964
  The exploring word. Cambridge, 1967
  English in Australia now. Cambridge, 1973
  English for meaning. NFER, 1980
Holmes, E. *What is and what might be*. Constable, 1911
Hourd, M. *The education of the poetic spirit*. Heinemann Educational Books, 1949
Hughes, T. *Poetry in the making*. Faber and Faber, 1969
Inglis, F. *The Englishness of English teaching*. Longmans, 1969
Koch, K. *Wishes, lies and dreams*. Chelsea House Publishers, 1970
Langdon, M. *Let the children write*. London, 1961
Leavis, F. R. *New bearings in English poetry*. Penguin, 1972
Marshall, S. *Creative writing*. Macmillan, 1974
Martin, N. (ed) *Writing and learning across the curriculum*. Ward Lock Educational, 1976
Mathieson, M. *The preachers of culture*. Allen and Unwin, 1975
Peel, M. *Seeing to the heart*. Hart-Davis, 1975
Pound, E. *ABC of reading*. Faber and Faber, 1961
Rosen, H. *The language of primary school children*. Penguin, 1973
Rosenblatt, L. *Literature as exploration*. Heinemann Educational Books, 1970
Sampson, G. *English for the English*. Cambridge University Press, 1975
Schayer, D. *The teaching of English in schools 1900–1970*. Routledge and Kegan Paul, 1972
Skelton, R. *Poetic Truth*. Heinemann Educational Books, 1978
  The poet's calling. Heinemann Educational Books, 1975
  The practice of poetry. Heinemann Educational Books, 1971
Stuart, S. *Say*. Nelson, 1969
Thompson, D. *Children as poets*. Heinemann Educational Books, 1972
Whitehead, F. *Creative experiment*. Chatto and Windus, 1970
  The disappearing dais. Chatto and Windus, 1971
Wilkinson, A. *The foundations of language*. Oxford University Press, 1971

SELECT BIBLIOGRAPHY 3

On Drama Teaching

Allen, J. *Drama in schools*. Heinemann Educational Books, 1979

Boulton, G. *Towards a theory of drama*. Longman, 1979

Cook, C. *The play way*. London, 1917

Grotowski, J. *Towards a poor theatre*. Eyre Methuen, 1976

Hodgson, J. (with Richards E): *Improvisation*. Eyre Methuen, 1966
  The uses of drama Eyre Methuen, 1977

Laban, R. *Modern Educational Dance*. MacDonald and Evans, 1975
  A Life for dance. MacDonald and Evans, 1975

McGregor, L. (with Tate and Robinson) *Learning through drama*. Heinemann Educational Books, 1977

Parry, C. *English through drama*. Cambridge University Press, 1972

Robinson, K. *Exploring theatre and education*. Heinemann Educational Books, 1970

Slade, P. *Introduction to child drama*. University of London Press, 1969

Wagner, B. J. *Dorothy heathcote: drama as a learning medium*. Hutchinson, 1979

Way, B. *Development through drama*. Longman, 1967